Guide to the American Liberal

A journey through the mind of the American
Progressive, Leftist, Lefty, Lib, Liberal

© 2011 Sal Iver

ISBN 978-0-615-52735-2

Guide to the American Liberal
by Sal Iver

PROLOGUE

This book is devoted to the American Liberal – that beacon of hope, praise, justice, light unto the future. Yes, Liberals present themselves as all this and more. Of course, for the rest of us the word irony comes to mind.

But there is so much more to this funny, fuzzy creature --- yes sooooo much more. Oooh, boy is there more!

No doubt the contributions from this venerable vessel of vitriolic vernacular are virtually endless – or is it virtuously endless as Liberals have come to never be wrong about anything. Even when admitting mistakes the Liberal has a way of making it appear as though that mistake was really the right path that was somehow subverted by mean people who just don't get it.

But then someone's not getting it is no obstacle to this venerable vessel, for he or she has shouting power and the ability to organize. And organize they do ... and shout ... boy can they shout.

American Liberals are very social. They love gatherings. They Facebook, Email, Text Message and Twitter until the power grids collapse, allowing their getting together in vast crowds and shouting. Do they do something about what they are shouting about? Please ... if they did then what would they get together to shout about?

In fairness we have to separate the American Liberal from his or her genetic aberration: The European Leftist. There are no

Liberals in Europe, only Leftists. What is the difference? The American Liberal shouts, marches, complains, rallies. Instead, European Leftists just riot, destroy, burn and steal. Unfortunately, sometimes the two mix to the detriment of our venerable Liberal.

There is one further thought for those Liberals who will inevitably get together in a rally to scream about this book. Over the past few decades the great Liberals of the past – the masters who gave us National Parks, child labor laws, paid vacations, workplace safety and so much more that bettered the lives of so many tens of millions of Americans are long gone. The current Liberal is just a cardboard replica who too often morphs into a singular being: the Libleftyprog, standing for the fusion of Lib, Liberal, Leftist, Lefty, Progressive. Were their forefathers to be transported to today they would collectively punch the lot of them in the choppers.

So we humbly present this fulgent formulator of fatuous factoids, this post promethean promulgator of palatine posturing: the American Liberal.

Travel with us on a journey through the mind of the American Progressive, Leftist, Lefty, Lib, Liberal.

"Think the Liberals will complain about this book?"

"They'll first have to make room in their busy schedule."

"What schedule?"

"Their busy schedule of things to complain about."

"Man, if this Global Warming gets any worse it'll take him a week to shovel out his walk."

1

"Who is that guy?"

"He was a scrawny 130 pound bank robber who bulked up using the ultra-gyms Liberals forced prisons to install."

"Why is that guy so angry?"

"He's a Democrat who was told by the Republican Senate leader that today is opposite day and it has him totally stymied."

"Why is that guy so glum?"

"He is a Democrat who voted for Obama's four billion dollar cut in heating oil for the elderly."

"Why'd he do that?"

"He still thought it was opposite day."

"Who's that guy?"

"He's a serial killer serving 50 life sentences who has been paroled early because the Liberals didn't like 'crowded' prisons."

"Who's that guy?"

"He's a serial killer who chopped up 50 people, but his case was dismissed because he wasn't read his Miranda Rights."

"Why is she running like that
and tossing away that gun?"

"She had to run out of her house after a molester
murderer broke in and threatened to kill her."

"Why?"

"God forbid if she shot him she could be
prosecuted for felony manslaughter."

7

1. "You don't understand! Bankers are stealing trillions of dollars a day from us! This is a great danger to our very safety! It's going to destroy us! We have to stop the Republicans."

"But didn't the Democrats start all of this and wasn't it Chris Dodd and Clinton who ......"

2.

1. "Now I promise you that we Progressives are going to write letters to our Congressmen demanding help for the disabled poor and the homeless and for more aid to soup kitchens."

2.

"That said, make sure you all join the rest of us on the Left for the 500 city ten million person march to support the BDS."

"What the heck is BDS?"

"The Boycott, Divest and Sanction movement by the Liberals to delegitimize Israel."

"Who's that guy?"

"He's a serial killer who chopped up 50 people, but his case was dismissed because his house was searched without a warrant after an officer selling Policeman Ball tickets noticed he was holding a human head."

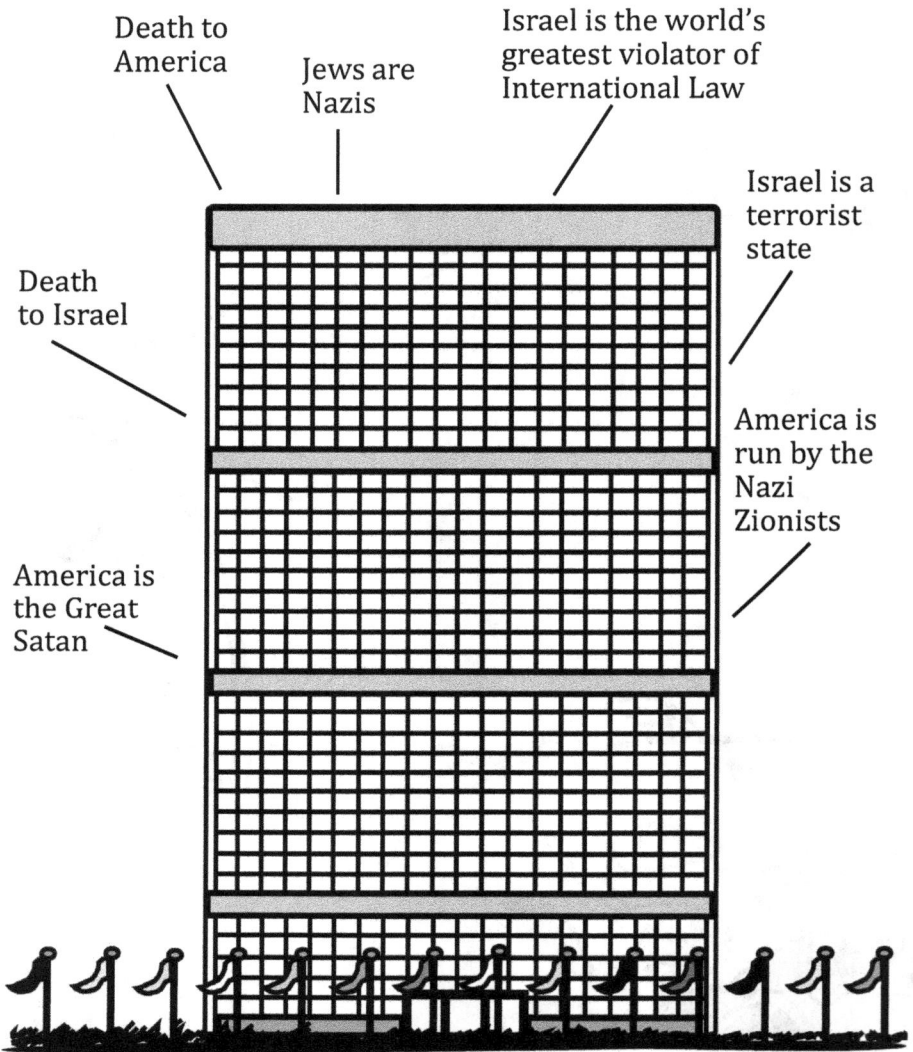

14

"Why isn't somebody doing something about this?"

"They are. These things have been put on the endangered species list."

"Isn't there something we can do?"

"Sure. Let them grow into the millions and then they'll come off the endangered species list."

17

"What in the world is he expecting to do with that contraption?"

"Based on the specs he should be able to power up his electric egg beater on windy days."

Great Windmill Park

"I thought Progressives loved birds."

"They do ... they do ... They uhhhhh love them to bits!"

"What in the world are those windmills doing so many miles off shore?"

"The Liberals wanted windmill energy sources, but they didn't want them to spoil their view."

"But don't the miles of underwater lines have great power losses and are very expensive?"

"Sure ... but to Libs that's the cost for getting cheap energy."

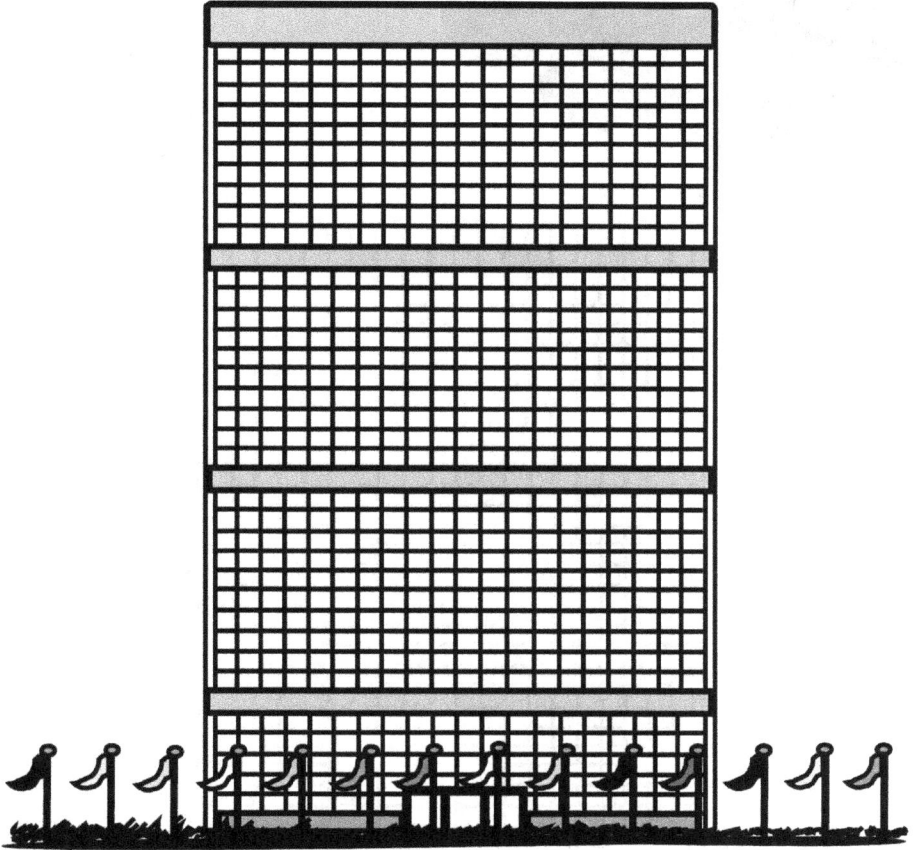

"Well, according to the Leftist yapping the UN is vital because giving a voice to all nations is a must to maintain peace and stability in the world."

"Wikipedia lists about 30 wars and conflicts currently underway in the world."

"Can't argue with success."

"Hmmmmm ... Can't think of anything else to say about the UN?"

"I can ... But it wouldn't be fit to print."

"But it would all be true."

"That's why the Libs wouldn't let it be printed."

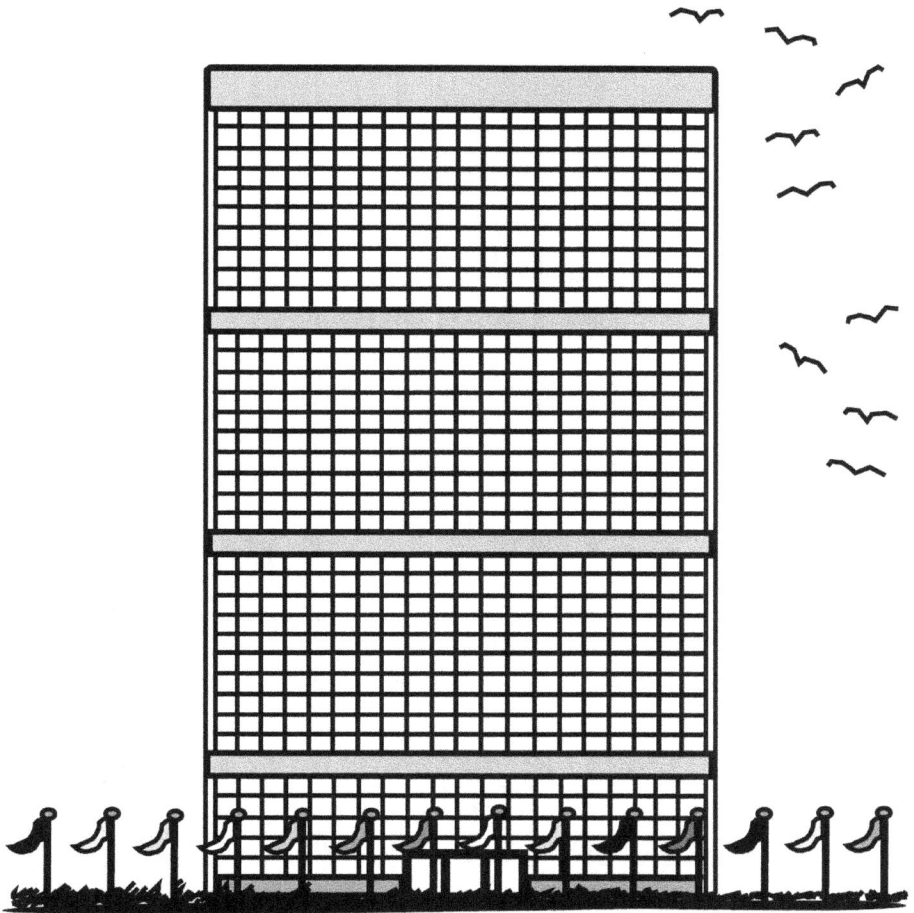

"Remember when John Bolton said
you can lose the top ten stories and
not make a difference?"

"Shows he knows nothing about
business. How about the Starbucks
stores and Nathan's Famous Franks
outlets? They'd go bust."

"I stand corrected. There
actually IS a use for the UN."

"Who's in that car?"

"Some famous Hollywood personality on her way to a Save-the-Planet rally to complain about our country's wasteful energy policies."

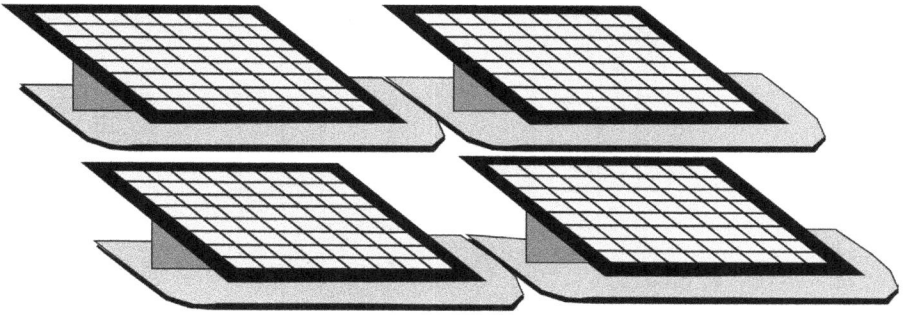

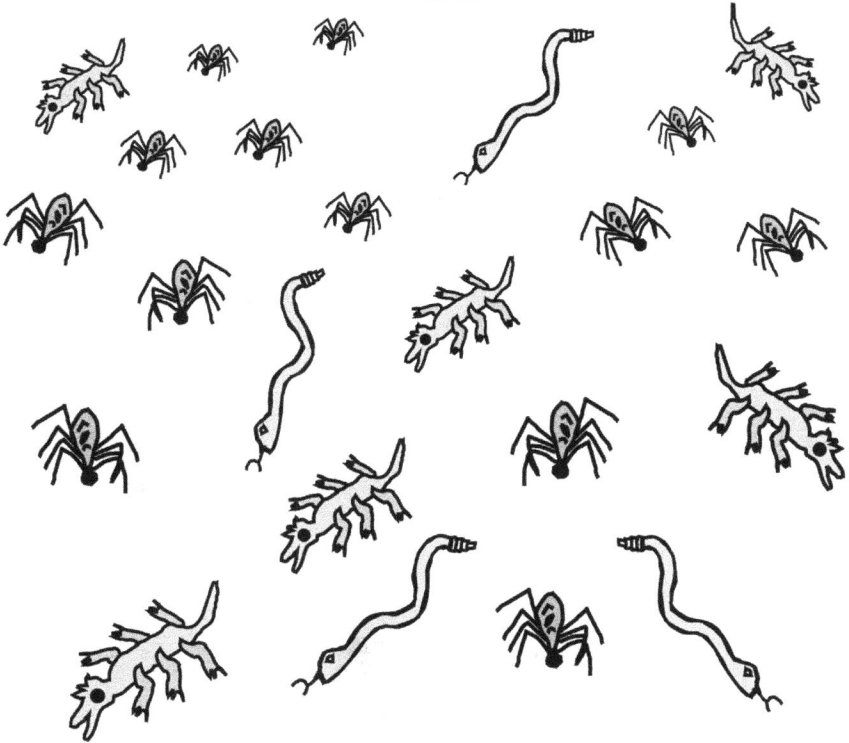

"Look at all those poor critters running for their lives.
I thought solar panels are ecologically friendly."

"Sure, if you don't mind living
in a thousand degree ecology!"

25

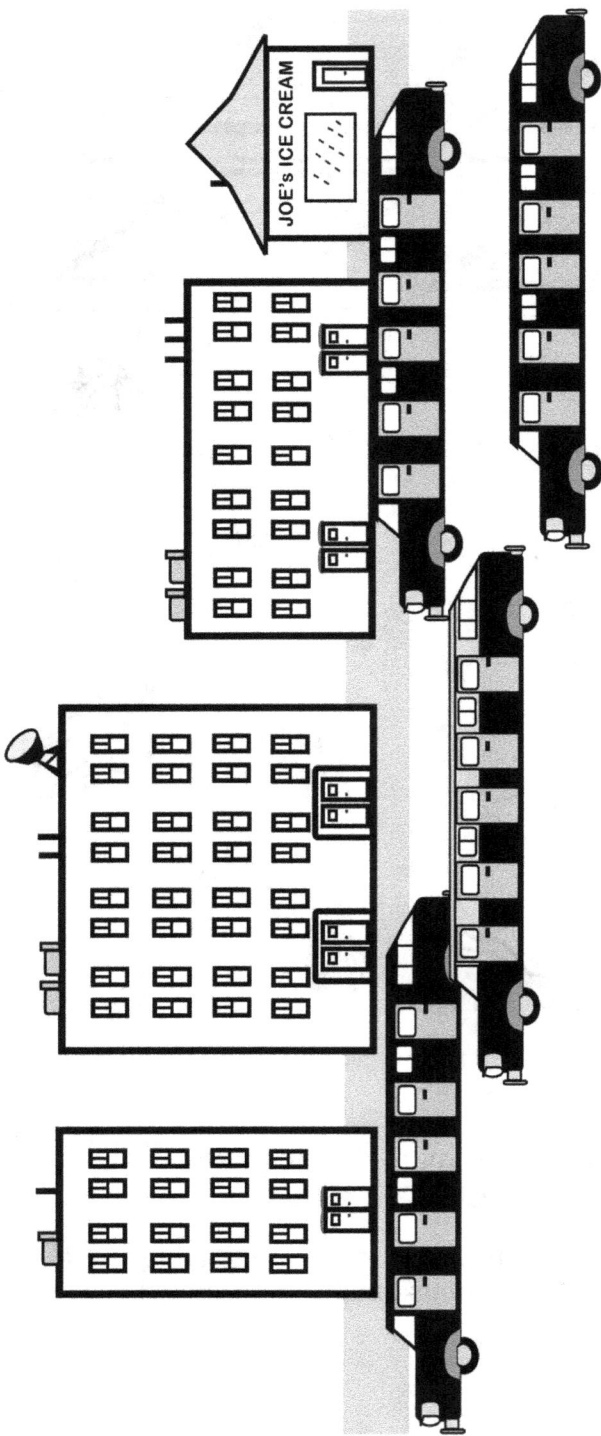

"Who's in those?"

"You know, big wig Liberals and Hollywood personalities on their way to a Save-the-Planet rally to complain about our country's wasteful energy policies."

"Ha! Don't they all also have 30-room houses that are air conditioned to 68 degrees?"

"I guess by freezing their houses they can cool off the earth? Sounds pretty progressive to me."

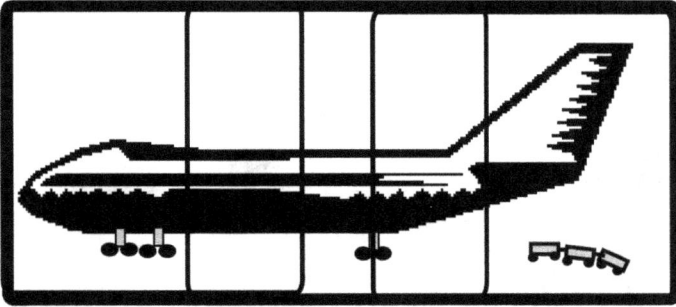

"How did those guys get through while the 90 year old nuns behind the gray curtain are being strip searched?"

"What! You want profiling?"

"DON'T YOU SEE! IT'S GLOBAL WARMING! YOUR FUTURE IS IN JEOPARDY BECAUSE THIS PLANET IS WARMING UP!"

"Yep ... It rains ... it doesn't rain ... it snows ... it doesn't snow. It's cold ... it's warm ... windy ... no wind. It's all Global warming. Why can't those folks over there get that through their heads?"

"You've hit the nail on the head. Just cool the place down a little and all will be fine with them."

"I don't get the Liberals. Why aren't they shoveling millions of dollars a year into this place?"

"They have been."

"What? What was this place like before they started doing that?"

"The same."

"Who's that guy?"

"He's a rabid anti-gun advocate."

"Why is he so heavily armed?"

"He's afraid if he gets attacked he's gonna need to be armed."

"Wow! How did that explosion happen?"

"Oh, that's caused by that ignorant, incompetent idiot at the control panel."

"Why wasn't he fired?"

"Yeah ... shoulda been ... but he's in the union."

31

"What's with that guy?"

"He's been tortured."

"I thought the Liberals are dead set against torture. So why do they do it?"

"It's their only way to find out if it works or not."

"I thought they hated Bush for it."

"Yeah, but they water boarded this guy 297 times to try to get him to admit it doesn't work."

"Who's that guy?"

"He used to be a normal guy, then he spent a day listening to the Progressives explain their opposition positions to everything the Conservatives do."

"Wh' ... why di' ... didn't we get a wa ... warning about this?"

"We did, but Al Gore and the leading scientists were screaming about a Global-Universal Interactive Event and nobody understood what they were talking about."

England: "We MUST stop Global Warming.
We Must stop polluters."

  China: "The United States has 4% of the world's
  population yet creates 25% of all pollution."

United States: "Hey, guys, you can't even see half the cities in
China through the smog, and England's green house gases are
rising in near double digit percentage rates."

  All Countries Shouting: "This may be true, but the
  United States has to lead the way or the 195 of the
  rest of us countries can't do anything!"

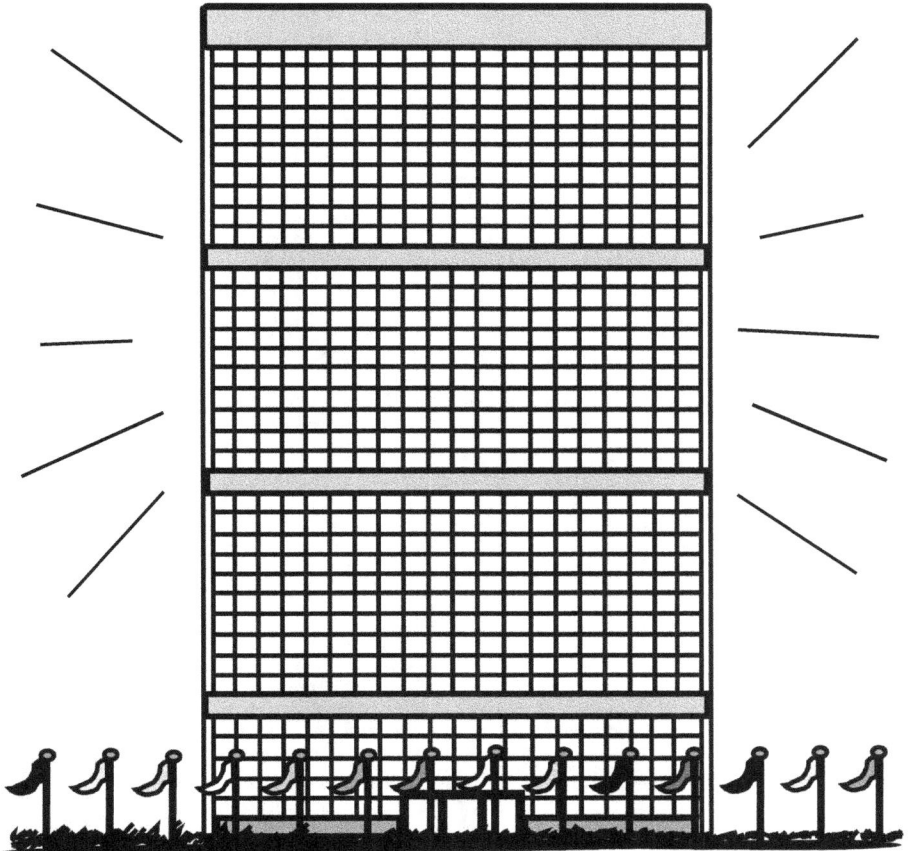

"I really have nothing to add to that."

"Ditto."

"The UN Human Rights Council
meeting will now come to order."

"Mr. Chairman, what is on the docket today?"

"Israel, of course."

"But the UN Secretary General has cautioned
that 92% of all of our efforts are geared towards
demonizing and sanctioning Israel."

"Your point is well taken. We must
redouble our efforts to get to 100%."

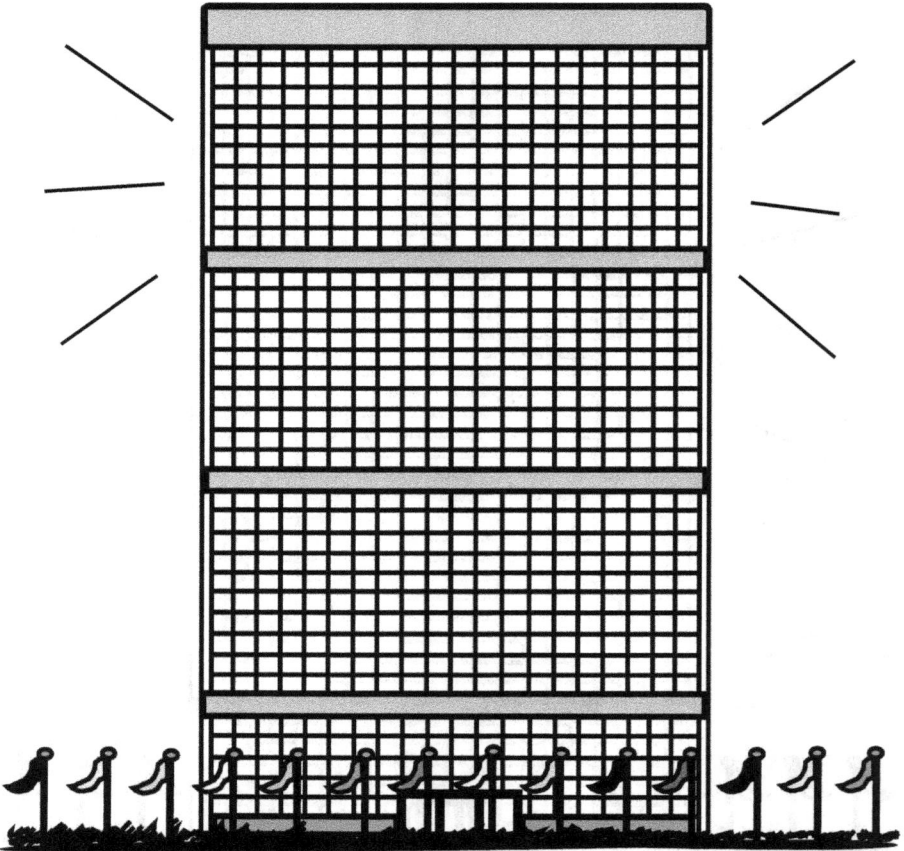

"Does 'oy vey' apply here?"

"Watch it or the Council will
find a way to sanction you."

Death to
Israel

Israel is Satan

Kill Jews

Jews hates
Muslims

Israel is a
terrorist
state

We all hate
America

Kill
America

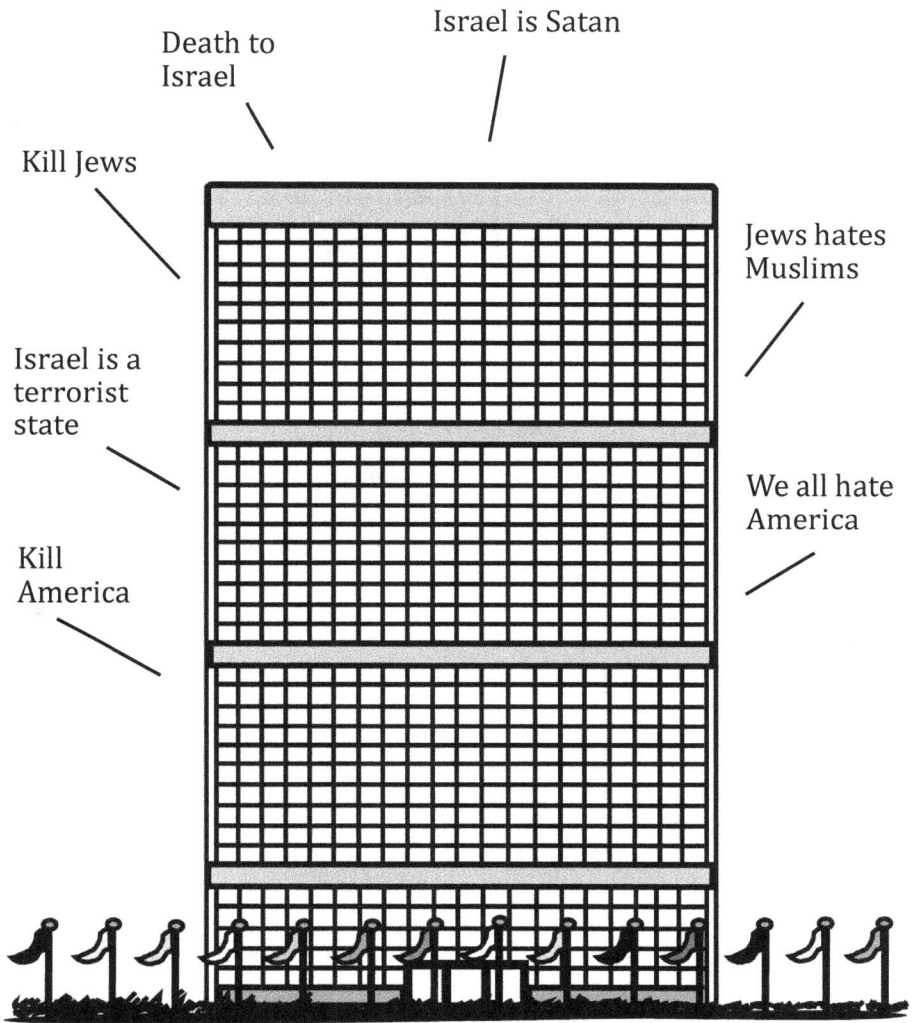

"Why does the UN spend so
much time focusing on Israel?"

"Well, the members have to balance out
the time they spend slamming the USA."

37

"Aren't those guys illegals from Mexico?"

"Yeah ... so?"

"Doesn't a leading Progressive in the movement against exploiting immigrants live there?"

"Yeah ... so?"

"Don't the people down there have poisons to stop those things?"

"Sure. But they are liberals and can't use the poisons."

"Why?"

"Something about hurting endangered tree thrips."

"Man are those people poor."

"Yeah ... It really is a shame."

"You mean it's such a shame people have to live this way?"

"Sure is. These people used to be in the Middle Class until Lib policies took all their money to support the poor."

"So what are the Libs doing now?"

"With no Middle Class left they're trying to tax the rich."

"I know. I know. He's a rabid anti-gun advocate."

"No, he' s just a Progressive who finally listened to himself speak and is trying to protect himself."

"From what?"

"Fellow Progressives."

"He looks important. Who is he?"

"A leading Liberal Democratic Senator screaming at the crowd that something has to be done about this."

"What's he planning to do?"

"Scream in Congress that something has to be done about this."

"Will he take action? He is a Senator."

"Nah ... Liberals like screaming. Doing something takes too much work."

"Why is the road to the right in such good shape?"

"A Democratic Congressman lives down there."

"I thought Democrats are supposed to be for the people."

"Yeah ... so long as the people are themselves and in power."

"I suppose a save-the-planet liberal lives there."

"How'd you know?"

"Well ... fireplaces produce all kinds of particles and carbon dioxide, right?"

"Yeah ... and?"

"Who but a save-the-planet liberal would run 8 fireplaces in a warm climate like this?"

"Are all of those people volunteers?"

"Of course!"

"But aren't these houses sold for a nice profit?"

"Sure."

"That's pretty funny."

"Maybe, but the joke is on those volunteers."

"All those homeless people. Where did they all come from?"

"Post another one in the Liberals' win column."

"What do you mean?"

"These were mainly people in psychiatric hospitals who were too sick to take care of themselves, and the Liberals decided hospitalization was inhumane."

"And they are better off rotting on the streets?"

"Like I said, 'Post another one in the Liberals' win column.'"

"I sure hope Global Cooling kicks in soon. I want to sit on my walk in January in a bathing suit, sipping piña coladas."

"Give that guy credit. Even in a world full of Liberals he still has hope."

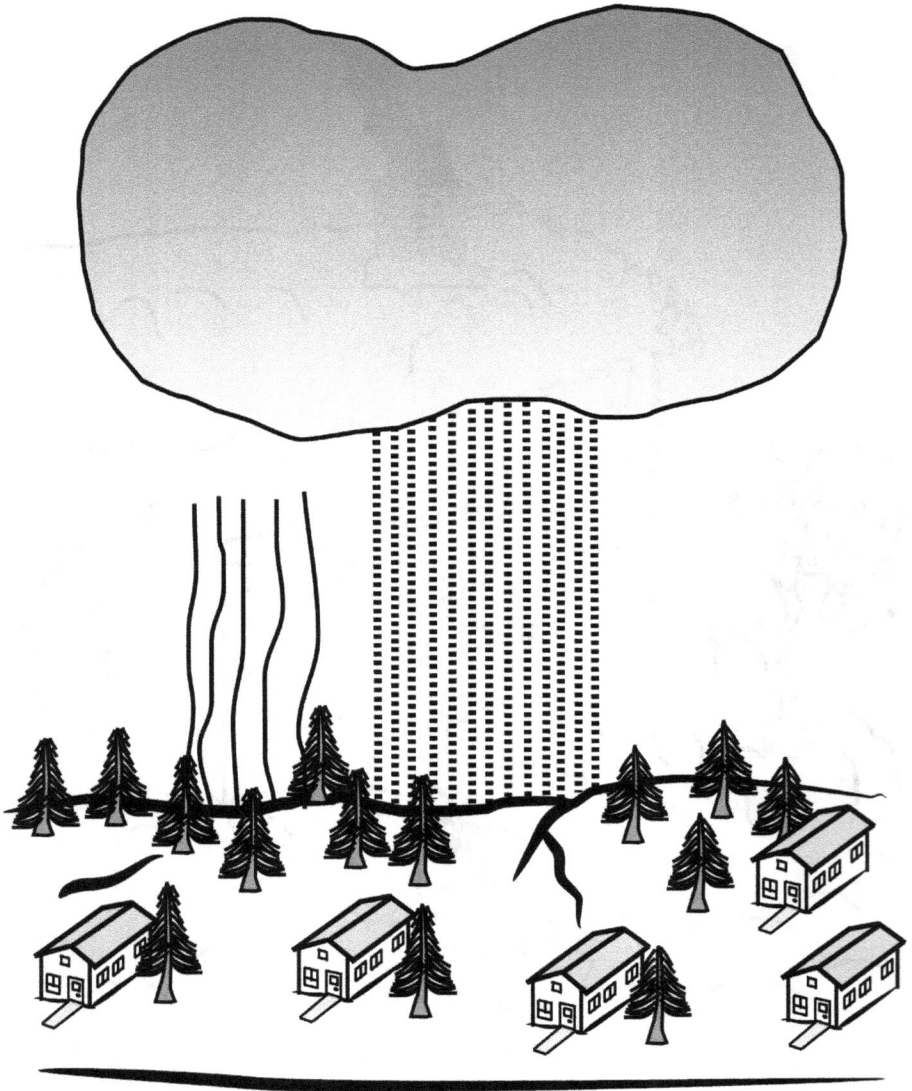

"Wow, that nuclear bomb must have killed 20 million people. What did today's news say?"

"Nothing. A dog saved a six year old blonde girl from tearing her dress on a fence and it knocked the nuclear attack completely off the news cycle."

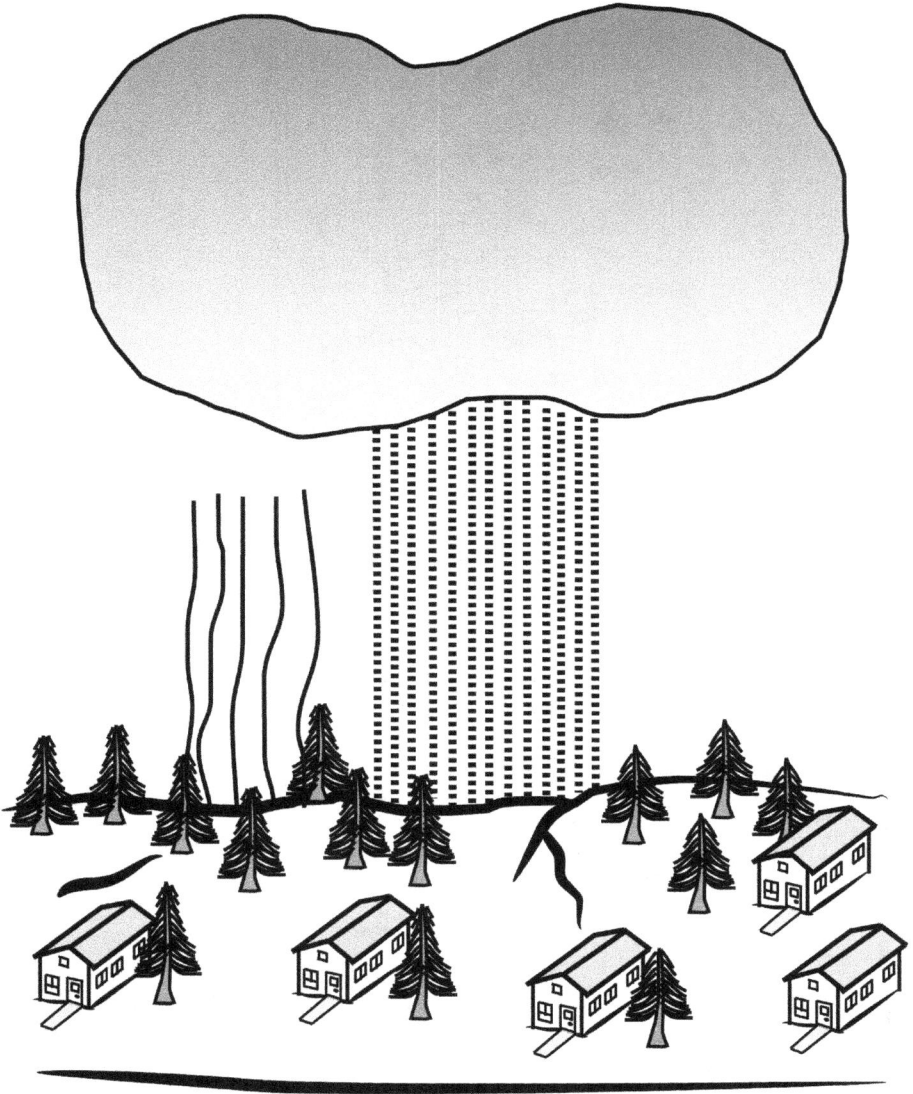

"Wow! Look at that bomb. Iran finally carried out its threat. How do you think the government will respond?"

"The Libs will make sure they start stacking up more nuns and old ladies in strip search lines at airports."

49

National Gay Pride Parade

Queers Against Israeli Apartheid

"Is that sign for real?"

"Sure. Why do you ask?"

"Isn't this about as ridiculous as the Left can get?"

"Nah. There's a lot worse nutty stuff waiting in the queue."

50

"BDS!
BDS!
BDS!"

"Apartheid!
Apartheid!"

"Israel is the world's
greatest violator of
International Law!"

"I know ... Those guys are Liberals
who have fallen on really hard times."

"Right ... but first they
fell on their heads."

51

National Gay Pride Parade

Queers Against Israeli Apartheid

"I don't get it. Aren't gays always complaining about how brutally society treats them?"

"Yeah. So?"

"So what's the purpose of this banner?"

"They're Leftists. Hating Israel ... it's a knee-jerk reaction for anyone on the Left."

"Shouldn't you leave out the word 'knee'?"

"Big Oil has us by the throat! Senators Glob and Blob are in the pocket of Big Oil!"

Blah Blah
Blah Blah
Blah Blah
Blah Blah
Blah Blah
Blah Blah

"Didn't those Senators get $26,000 each for their campaigns?"

"Yeah ... but each one spent 7 million bucks to get elected."

"Yup ... Big Oil with its deep pockets is on the road to owning us all."

"Aren't the super rich Lefties aware of this horrible poverty existing here in the United States?"

"Sure they are."

"So what are they doing about it?"

"Sending their money to feed the poor in Africa."

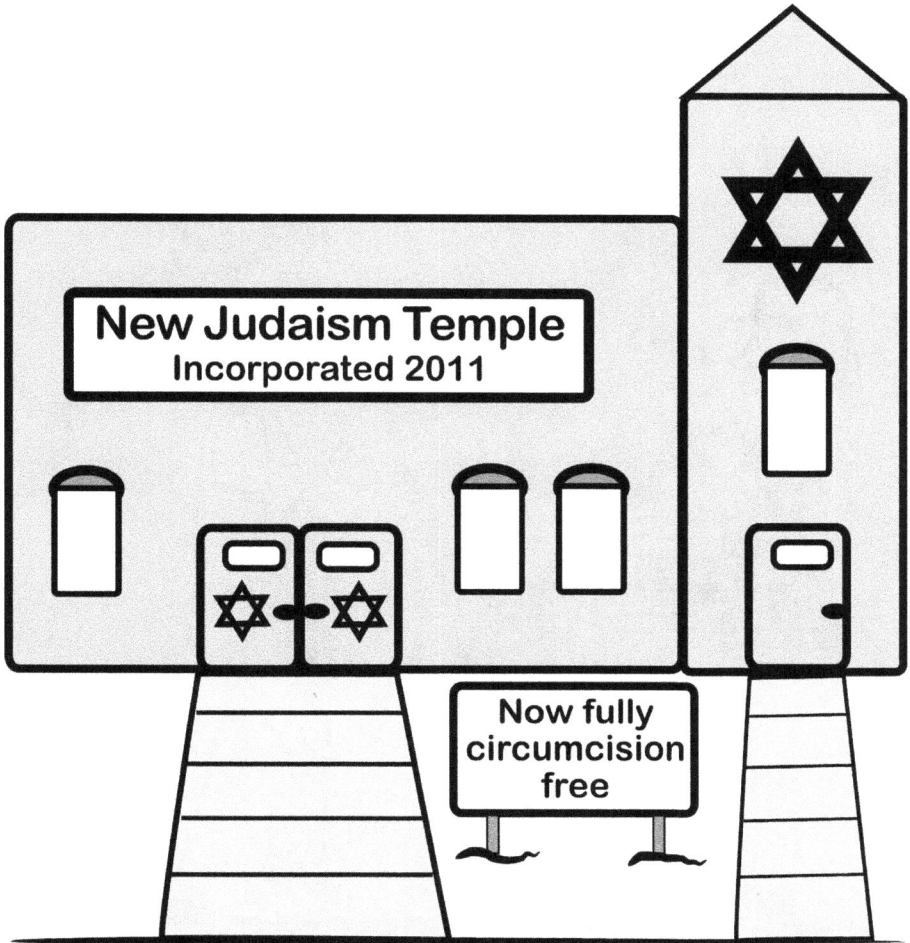

"Isn't circumcision considered worldwide to be very effective against sexually transmitted diseases and is a safe procedure and a religious ritual for over a billion and a half people?"

"Yeah ... been around a few thousand years, too."

"So why did the Libs suddenly stick their noses into this and pass laws against it?"

"Must be if it has any relationship to religion it must be bad and has to be banned."

55

"What's his problem?"

"Oh ... he's a typical Lib panicking over what to call that guy: African American, Native American, Afro-Native American, Nativo-Africa man ... whatever."

"What if he just calls him 'Sir'?"

"What! And risk being politically incorrect!"

Liboleft Elementary School

"Tag ... You're it! You're not it! We are all it and all not it."

"Isn't this carrying the Liberal policy that all kids are equal to an extreme?"

"Ha! Wait until you see them try playing football."

57

"Hey, here's a good joke. A Polish-American, a Mexican-American and a man of Caucasian heritage enter into an establishment which has a main purpose of selling alcoholic beverages ..."

"Wow ... This man is really over-politically correct."

"Yeah? Think that's overboard? Wait for the ten-minute punch line!"

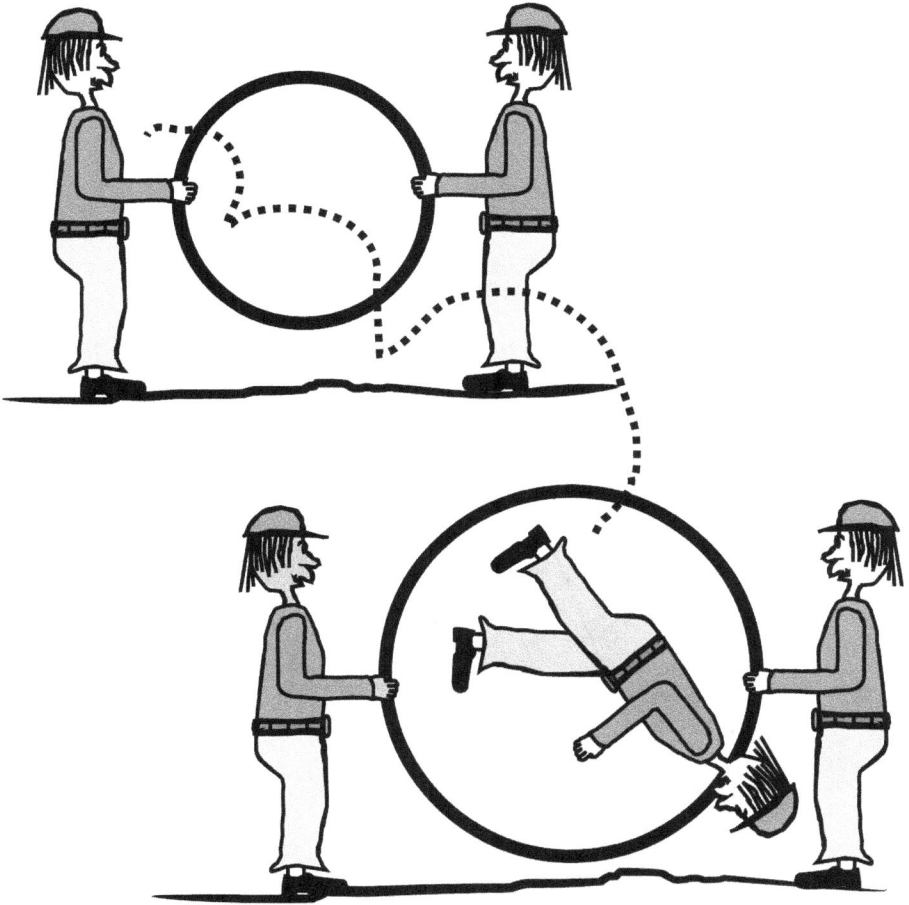

"Why is that man jumping through those hoops?"

"He's a Liberal."

"I get it. He takes everything literally."

"Look at that amazing mansion. Who lives there?"

"Some person who choked on a chicken bone and got her lawyers to sue all chicken companies for tens of millions of dollars."

"Shouldn't there be some kind of controls on the ease of filing such silly lawsuits?"

"Trying to make a living through filing frivolous lawsuits is a basic tenent of Liberalism."

"What caused all that garbage?"

"The Left held a Save the Planet rally last week."

"How come they didn't clean up their horrendous mess?"

"No time. They had to save the planet somewhere else."

"Why did everything die here?"

"The Liberals diverted all the water to feed their homes, swimming pools and automatic lawn sprinklers in California, Arizona and Nevada."

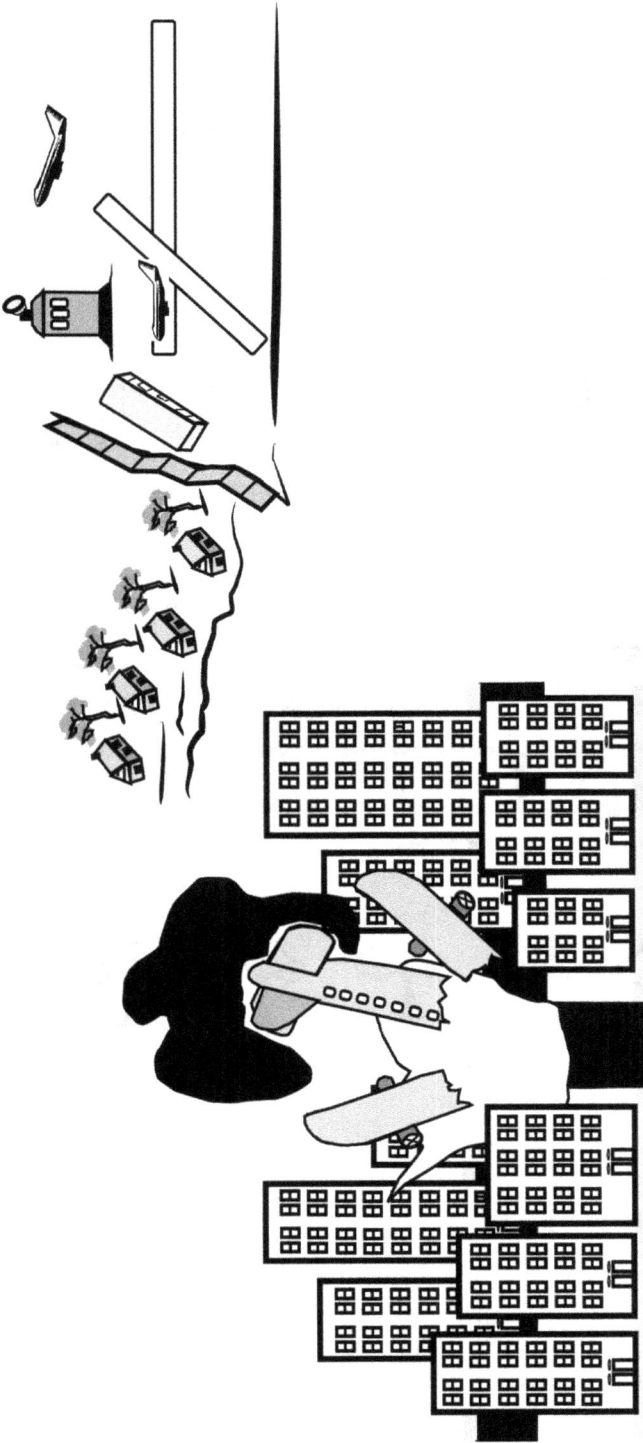

"Why are all those planes crashing?"

"The Libs jumped in and passed laws making the planes take off slower and quieter."

"Why?"

"Their noise on take-off was too loud and bothered the people who intentionally moved next to the airport."

"What are those incredibly tiny cars doing on the road?"

"Those three hundred pound cars are the Liberal answer to the oil crisis."

"We must stop off shore drilling!
It's destroying the environment."

"Don't we have, like, 50,000 of those rigs
out there built over the past 40 years?"

"And your point is?"

"So why is he so riled up over the spill from one
rig and didn't say a word for the past 40 years?"

"Like all Libs he was too involved
in enjoying all the benefits oil gave
to his lifestyle."

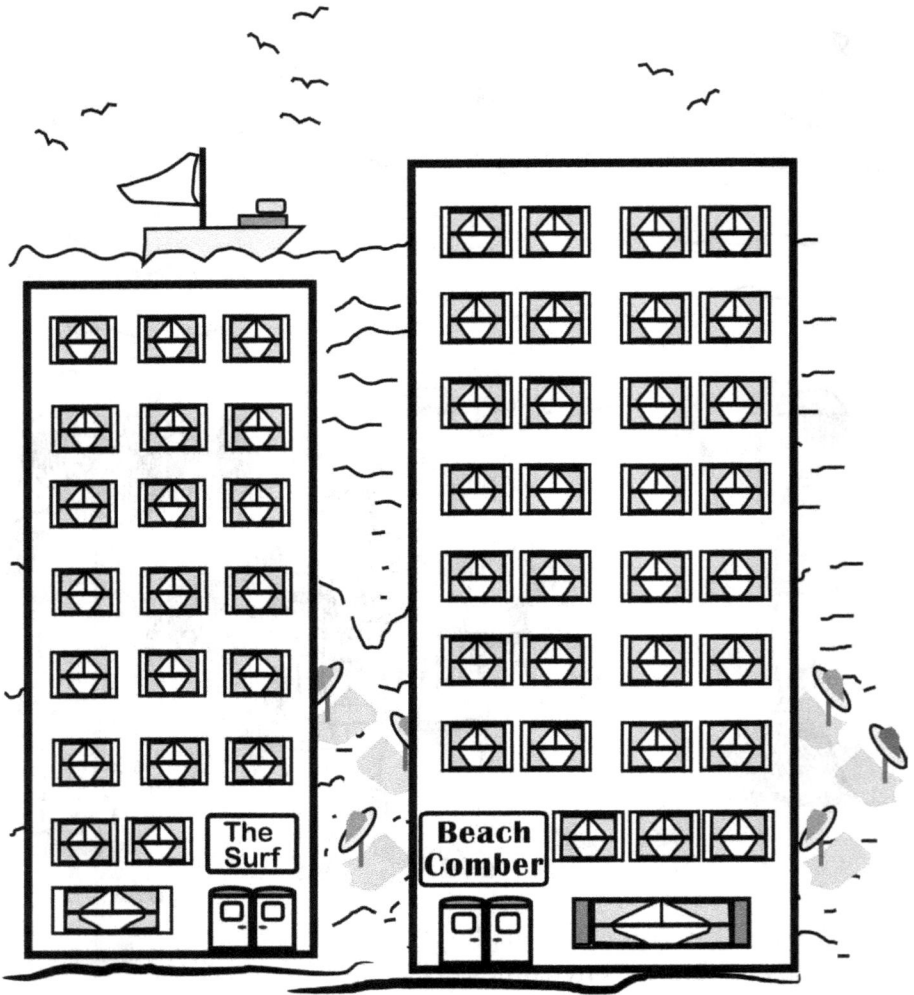

"Look at the size of those condos! They go on for miles almost completely blocking the view of the ocean. Who would do such a thing?"

"Those are Lib Yuppies living there."

"Why?"

"So they could get a view of the ocean."

"This seems to be a pattern all over the place. Poor people's houses torn down and the people moved who knows where."

"It's a good thing the Democrats are so concerned about them."

"Why? What are they going to do?"

"They're working on a non-binding resolution in Congress protesting all this."

"Look at all those poor people losing their homes."

"Yeah ... I sure feel sorry for them. There is nothing they can do to stop this"

"Don't they have all the Liberals on their side?"

"That's why I feel sorry for them."

Art for All ... All for Art

"I don't understand art, but I know what I like. And I don't like that."

"Why?"

"Then you can't ever be a Liberal."

"Because Liberals also don't understand art, but freedom of expression means anything and everything is art."

"So ... I guess the $250,000 spent on these didn't make this expression free for us taxpayers."

"Egads! That artwork is horrible. It looks like a junkyard. Who ordered that crap?"

"The County Art Commission. They paid two artists $250,000 to do that."

"That ... that was supposed to be part of the city improvement project?"

"Well ... it improved the finances of two really bad artists."

"What's behind that gigantic wall?"

"A gated neighborhood of ultra-rich Yuppie Liberals."

"What's it for? To reduce noise coming from the road down here?"

"Nah ... the Libs couldn't stand looking at the poor people, so they built that wall to block the view."

"You know, this road project has been going on for so long nobody can remember when it started."

"Some people can remember."

"Who?"

"The union bosses who are making sure they milk every nickel from every penny originally allocated for this job."

"I hear the union is soon
to be kicked off this job."

"Really? Why?"

"The Japanese have invented a
shovel that can stand by itself."

1.

"I want to introduce you to the good news about our Lord Jesus and ..."

2.

"For crying out loud! I can't stand people who knock on my door to sell me something! Get outta here!"

"But watch what happens next when a Lib comes to his door."

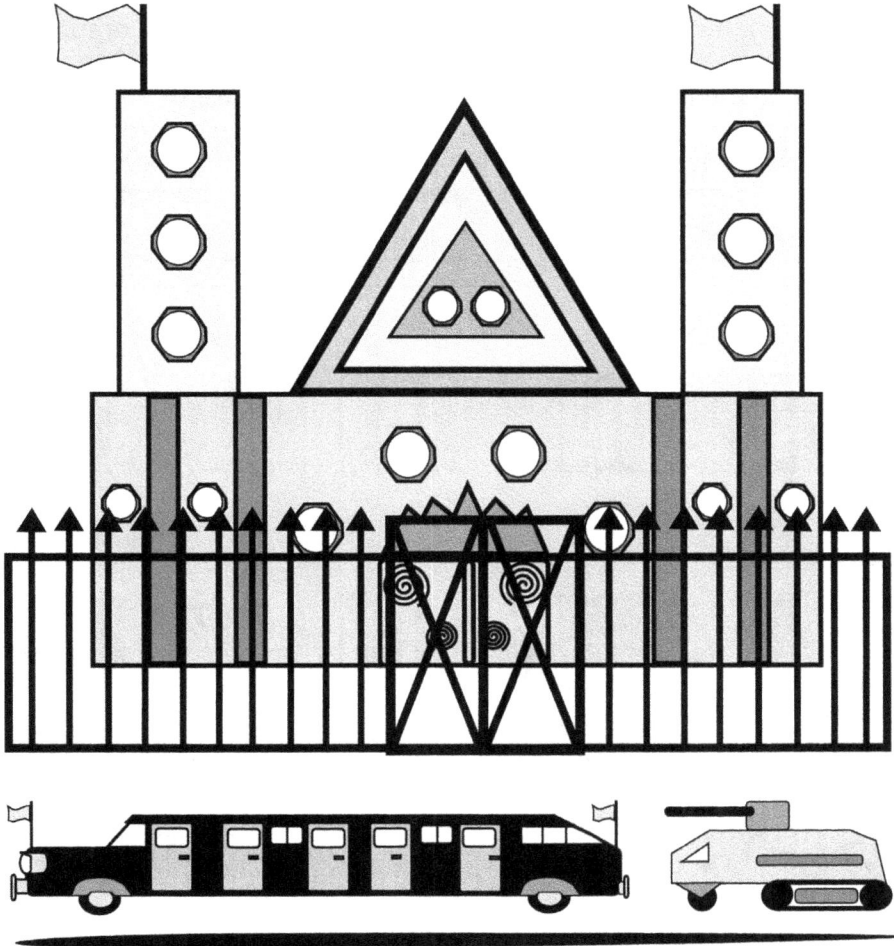

"How in the world did
that dictator get so rich?"

"Remember all those billions of
dollars that were sent to help his
country's poor and starving?"

"It all went to make him and his
cronies wealthy beyond belief?"

"Well ... the Libs still believe."

1. "My name is Don Radzilov and I own a full service company that can weed, feed and mow your lawn, trim your shrubs, do all edging and mulching. And our prices are the best in the area and we are fully insured – here's our insurance document – and have a 100% satisfaction guarantee."

2. "Ya know, Honey ... These slimy door-to-door creeps. Why don't they get a job! Uhhh ... by the way, honey, did you send in our donation to the United Way Food Stamps program?"

"It's hard to believe that a super rich
Lib still lives there after he made it big."

"He doesn't. He's just keeping
that house for convenience
when he visits old friends."

"He always brags about supporting
America, so where does he live now?"

"Well, he owns estates and villas in
Cannes, France ... Vancouver, Canada
... Paris ... London ... Venice ..."

"Who owns that? It must
cost fifty million bucks."

"A rich Lib who cries about
US jobs going overseas."

"So where did he buy that?"

"Italy."

"I know who owns that monster. He's a wealthy Lib who constantly screams that the rich don't pay their share of taxes."

"He doesn't even live in this state, so why is he docked here?"

"He found out by registering his yacht in this state he can avoid paying taxes."

"That high school costs fifty thousand bucks a year."

"Who goes there?"

"Wealthy Yuppie Libs send their kids there."

"Aren't those the same people who are always preaching how we must support public education?"

"And your point is?"

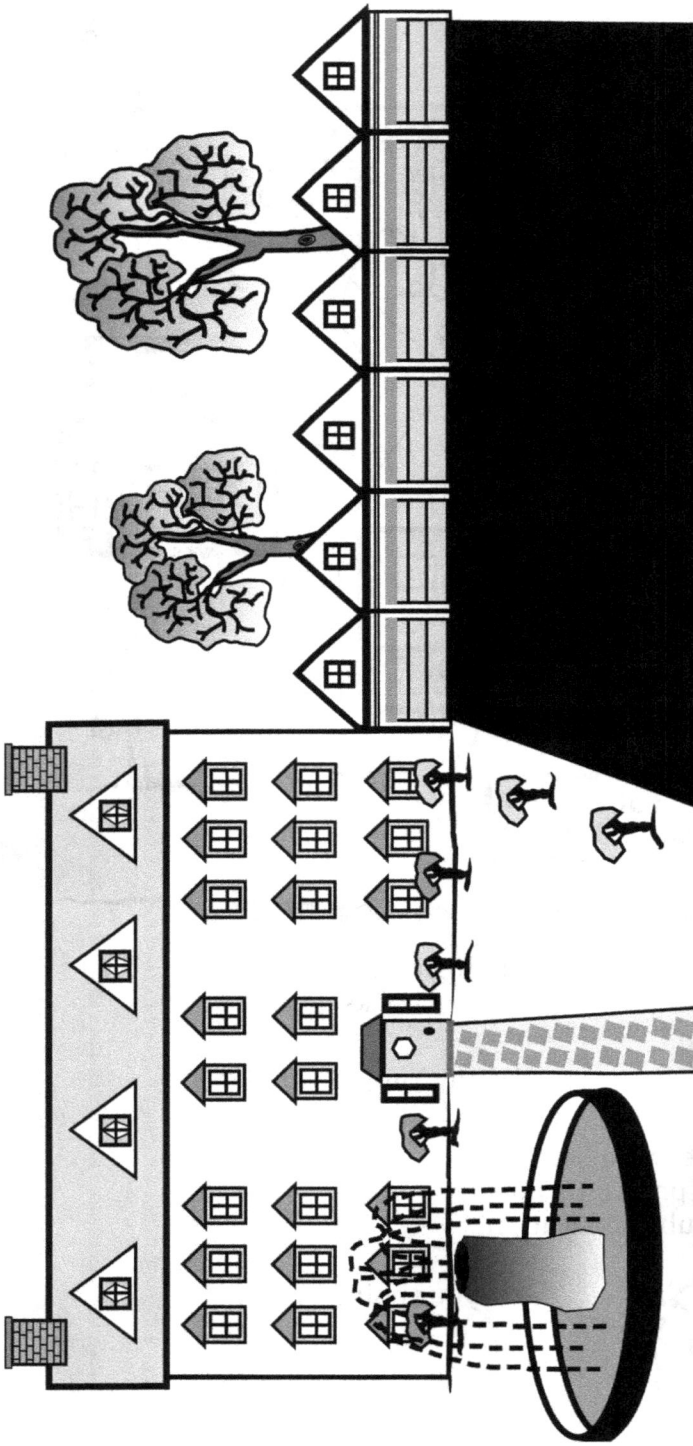

"I must say when Liberals get money they sure know how to live in style."

"What happened to their saving the world's resources?"

"Still there. They just want the rest of us to make up for their waste."

84

"That strike has been going on now for five months."

"They won't give in until all jobs are guaranteed and nobody can be fired."

"Won't that force the company to shut down this plant and move out of state?"

"Makes sense, though. If you don't have a job you can't be fired."

"Sounds like win-win to me."

"Who's that poor fellow?"

"He was a reporter there for thirty years and just got fired."

"Why?"

"He made the mistake of calling an African American a Black person."

"Who's that poor fellow?"

"He was a reporter there for thirty years and just got fired."

"Why?"

"He was seen saying hello to a prominent Conservative."

"Poor guy. He only started a few months ago and the union forced him out."

"Wh ... Why?"

"He broke the cardinal rule: never do more work than the laziest and most useless clown on the floor."

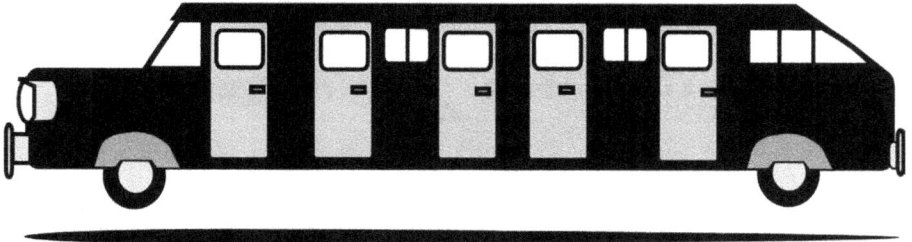

"Wow. He must have really hit it big."

"No. He's on food stamps."

"Huh? How'd he pay for that limo?"

"Food stamps."

"Hold it! Isn't that illegal? Who would so violate the law and sell a limo for a zillion food stamps?"

"Another Liberal."

"I swear I've never seen him work."

          "He does."

"Huh?"

          "He works just long enough to collect unemployment compensation."

"How long can he keep that up?"

          "Don't know, but thanks to Lib oversight he is now into his ninth year."

"Hey, John. I don't understand it. When are they going to plow this street? The snow is two and a half feet out there."

"Didn't you hear?"

"What?"

"The town crews unionized this year and their contract won't let them touch snow once it gets above six inches."

"So what are we supposed to do?"

"Wait for it to melt to below six inches."

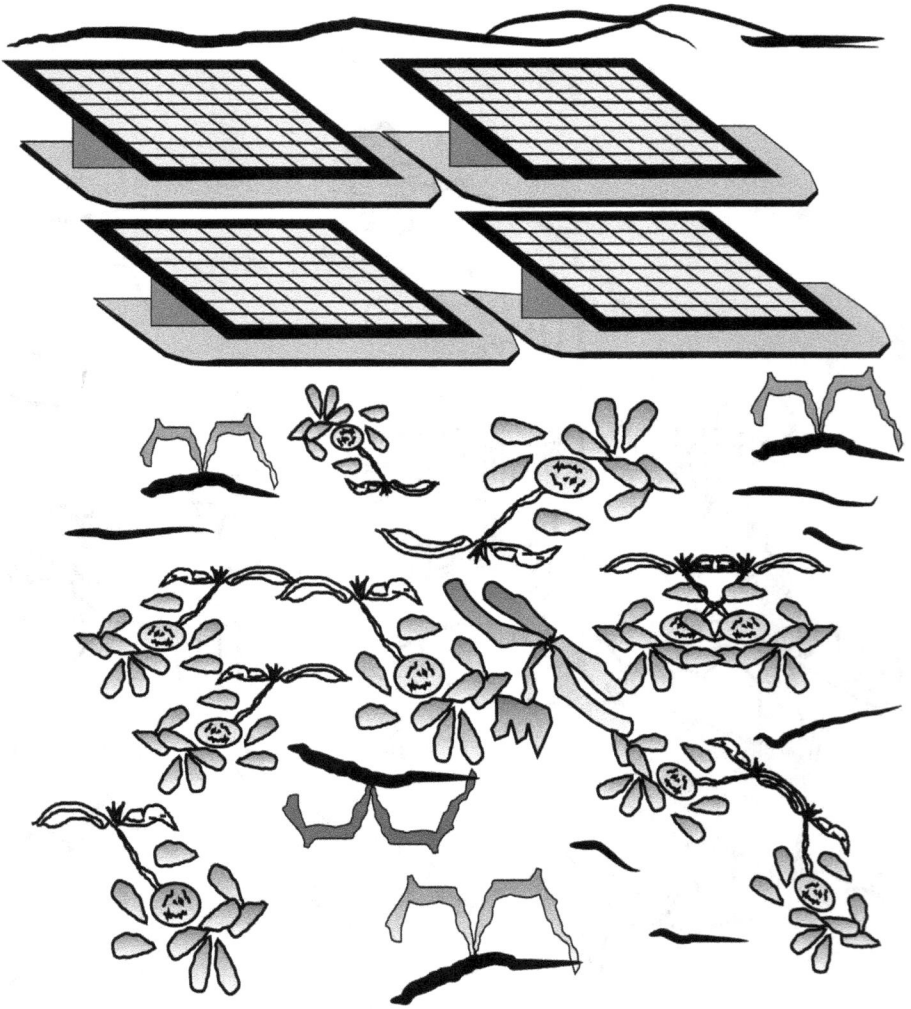

"Those solar panels are killing all the foliage for miles around."

"But think of all the ecologically friendly energy we are getting."

"But there are no electrical grid towers for miles."

"Hence the saving of the eco system. No power? No consumption. No destruction."

Great
Windmill
Park

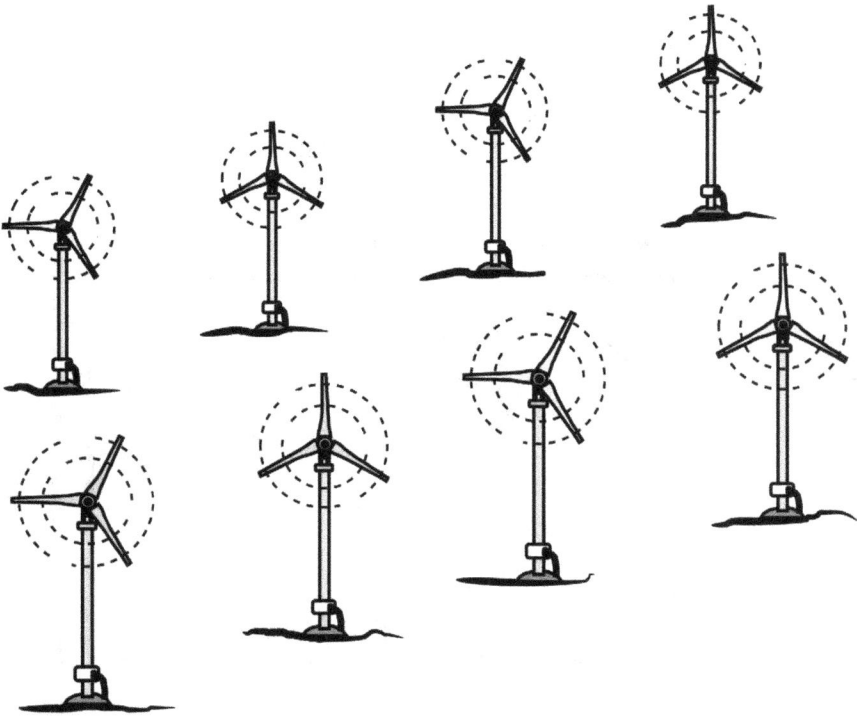

"How are these things supposed
to work when there is no wind."

"Not to worry. The liberals
complain so much these things
are going to be spinning 24/7."

"The Conservative agenda is destroying the Middle Class. It's tax policies favor only the rich!"

Liberal News Network

"Hold it. Didn't the Libs raise taxes on the Middle Class for 40 years to pour money into their social programs for the poor?"

"Yeah ... and the only Middle Class tax reductions ever came from the Conservatives."

"So ... "

"You got it! The Libs love the Middle Class to death!"

"The Conservative war machine is bankrupting this country, isn't it?"

"Of course. The Conservatives stand alone with their support for wars and don't even care if Congress agrees or not."

Liberals Sound Off

"Hoo boy. Wasn't it just a few years ago that nearly every Lib in Congress voted for our wars in the Middle East?"

"And don't forget, we also attacked Libya under Obama without Congress even having a say."

"Boy ... so what's the difference between a Conservative's war and a Liberal's war?"

"Liberals don't complain about their own wars."

"We have in our studio Dr. Ima Loudmouth. Ima, would you please explain how the Conservative economic policies are hurting our country? And how they're making us a second class country?"

"Thanks for having me. If you look at the banking regulations and how the Conservatives removed them and won't reinstate any controls ..."

Liberal News Network

"So, the Big Libs under Clinton removed the last controls, allowing the banks to act as they wish. So why didn't the Libs reinstate them if this bothered them so much?"

"Funny story here. The Dems from 2008 to 2010 held the greatest majority in the House and the Senate in the history of this country – the entire history of this country – including a filibuster proof lead in the Senate."

"So what happened?"

"They were powerless to do anything."

"Look at the devastation Hurricane Blob did. These people have no food, water, shelter ... and there are thousands and thousands of them. Thank Heaven we have the Liberals."

"Why? What are the Libs gonna do?"

"What they always do in a major crisis: Complain about these conditions on talk shows and send a hundred million bucks to Africa."

"Think of it. There are millions of dollars of art up there."

"It all looks like worthless crap to me."

"But it's art and according to Liberals who are you to decide what is and isn't art?"

"For one thing I'm the idiot who paid twenty bucks to come here thinking I was going to see art."

"The Conservatives are out to destroy Medicare, the most successful health care program in the world."

Liberal News Network

"I'm confused. Doesn't Medicare fraud soak up about sixty to eighty billion dollars a year? Enough, the Libs claim, to be able to fund a universal health care program?"

"Sure it does."

"So why don't the Libs crack down on this fraud?"

"What? ... Because they don't want to hurt the Americans most in need."

"I'm even more confused now."

"The Tea Party wants to cut everything we Liberals believe in."

"Yeah ... they're putting out and passing every bill under the sun."

"What should we do?"

"We must get our leadership to pass a non-binding resolution demanding we take a stand."

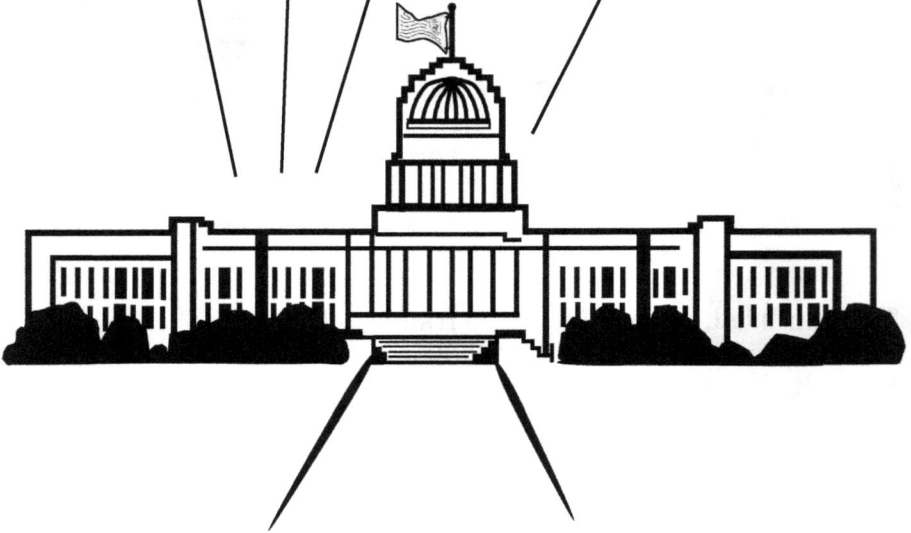

"Seems like the Liberals have their act together."

"Yep ... can't wait for their non-binding resolution on non-binding resolutions."

"There is part of our 800 billion dollar work projects and economic recovery money at work."

"Glad the money is at work. Seems like nobody on the job is working."

"How come whenever a large construction project is funded only unions can take part?"

"How else can you guarantee that a job can pay four times as many workers needed for five times as long as it was contracted for?"

"Why is this page totally blank?"

"For fairness we had to include a page totaling all the things the Liberals have done for us in the past 30 years."

103

"Why in the world is he digging all those holes?"

"He's been awarded a works project contract from the economic recovery money the Liberals pushed for."

"You mean the money that is ... uhhh ... only to go for shovel-ready projects?"

"Dearly beloved friends and family, we are here gathered to join in Holy matrimony William Goat to Katherine Blarge ..."

"Is this what the Conservatives warned would happen with Gay marriage?"

"Of course not. It's just that after hearing it said the Liberals figured since the Conservatives hated it, it must be OK."

"Obviously lawyers."

"So the guy behind him is the lawyer?"

"No ... the guy in front is chasing that ambulance because it brushed him while driving by."

"You catch on fast."

"Look at that house! Remember that guy running after the ambulance with the lawyer behind him?"

"And ..."

"And he sued every ambulance manufacturer and EMT service in the country."

"Why did he win that case?"

"The juries were all Liberals."

"What happened there?"

"That woman ran her gas barbecue grill inside despite big red warnings all over telling her not to."

"Man, she's skeerewed for sure."

"Nope. Her son is a lawyer and he's already suing that ten twelve-inch red square warnings wasn't enough."

"Oh, he'll lose that one."

"Don't think so. He already won her $150,000 because she drove her car into her kitchen because the manual didn't tell her not to."

"Why is that car still sticking out of that tree?"

> "Poor gal ... she beeped her horn and the tree didn't move so she sued the US Department of Forestry for not training its trees properly."

"By the looks of the house she won hands down."

> "Not totally. She got thousands of bucks, but the Forestry folks forced her to leave the car there as a warning to other trees."

"I take it the Forestry folks are Liberals?"

> "No, the Federal Circuit Court judges are."

"Dearly beloved friends and family, we are here gathered to join in Holy matrimony William Goat to the newly free Katherine Blarge ..."

"Let me guess. The Liberals are just carrying things too far."

"In a way. The Liberal local court allowed her to divorce her horse to clear the way for the goat."

"Dearly beloved friends and family, we are here gathered to join in Holy matrimony Katherine Blarge to both of these ..."

"You know, the Conservatives were attacked by the Liberals for being racist and bigoted for saying Gay marriage would lead to beastiality, bigamy, monsterality."

"With the Libs everything the Conservatives say is a challenge to them."

"That's why the bigamy?"

"You really do catch on fast."

"Yaargh! Who's that guy and why is he free?"

"He's a serial killer who slaughtered 30 people but got off on an insanity plea."

"So why isn't he in an asylum?"

"He was for three years, but a group of bleeding heart Liberals got the psychiatric board to announce he has been cured."

"Man ... I hope their hearts are the next to bleed!"

"Today Republican Senator Grub admitted to a sex scandal with a forty year old aid ..."

Liberal News Network

"Now there's a case those Lib lawyers and the media can jump all over."

"Gotta go where the real crime affecting us all is happening."

"Today a judge in Blug Township ruled against a restraining order for a woman who has been trying to free herself from a husband who has twenty wives. The Liberal judge ruled the husband had rights under Freedom of Religion ..."

Liberal News Network

"There are now a number of localities looking the other way on multiple wives based on one religious claim or another. How come the Liberals don't say a word about this? Aren't women supposed to be protected in marriage?"

"To the Liberals having many wives is just another form of freedom of expression."

"Huh? What? I thought Women's Liberation is a big cause for ... uhhhhh ... Liberals."

"Yeah. For women. But what's that have to do with the fun of a man having many wives?"

115

"Now isn't this really carrying the Liberal policy that all kids are equal to an extreme? Every kid is a valedictorian."

"Not really. The class has 682 students."

"So what happened to those remaining three?"

"Well ... somebody had to pay the price to show there was balance in the school's decision making."

"Why are all those poor people going into that tent?"

"They are part of the Liberals' Big Tent philosophy."

"How come there are no Middle Class people represented."

"They're the ones being forced to pay for the tent."

"Wow. That guy must be important. He was shot three times, overdosed on four types of drugs, fell off the roof of a building he was robbing and so far he has been given $450,000 in free medical care."

"Nah. He's a simple five-time loser thug taking advantage of the free health care that doesn't exist."

"Who is he?"

"He's a murderer on death row who is scheduled to be executed early next week."

"So why has he been given over $500,000 worth of medical treatment – heart transplant, liver transplant."

"Hey, whaddaya want? The Libs to deny him the best in health care?"

"What the heck happened here?"

"A peace march happened."

"Holy ... How did that happen?"

"While the TSA security people were busy strip searching and patting down every part of those hot girls from the USA beach volleyball team, five Middle Eastern terrorists ran by with bombs strapped on them."

TSA's ⟨**Hottest**⟩
Passengers of August

**Magazines
&
Beer**

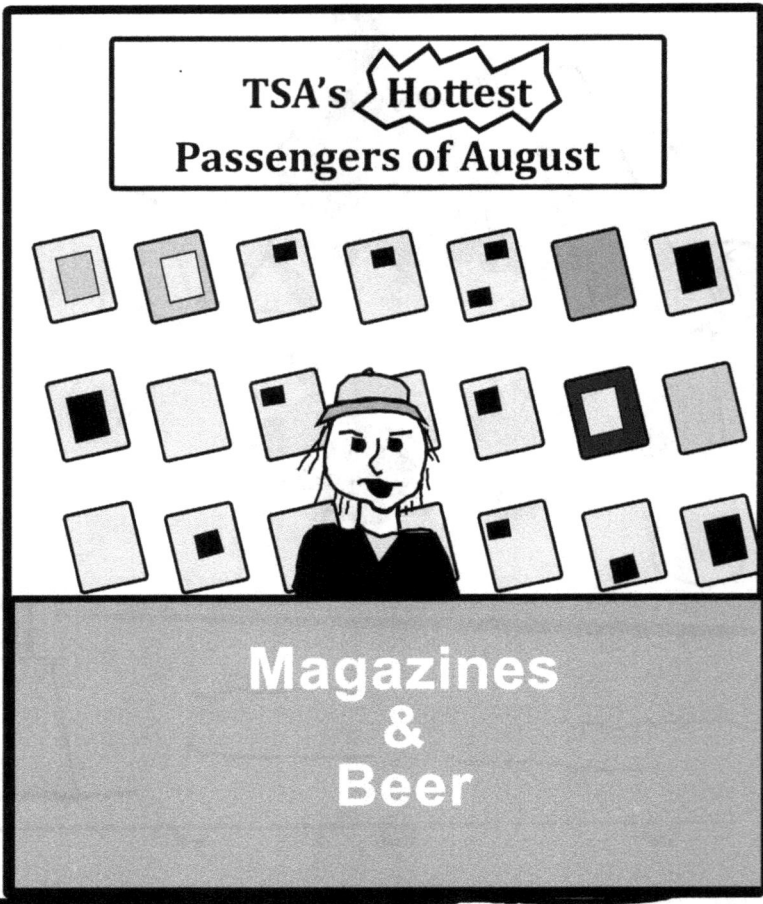

"So I guess it's safe to say the airport security body imaging machine photos aren't dumped at the end of each day."

"Sure they are. They're dumped into Hustler, Playboy, Penthouse, Facebook, YouTube ..."

"I thought the Libs stopped all this from happening."

"Who do you think's reading all this stuff."

"Today Republican Senator Flubber Margle was caught having sex with his aid. Two other aids have come forward charging Senator Margle with having sex with them, including a threesome."

Liberal News Network

"The Liberal media has been chewing his butt off on this one."

"Hold it. Didn't the Liberals and Lefties start the free sex movement, including wife swapping, premarital sex and large orgies?"

"That's one of the problems with the Left: They don't play well with others different from themselves."

"Yeah ... Gotta give it to them, though. They built their houses on good farm land and had trees cut down all over the vast acreage."

"As you said earlier: The Left doesn't play well with others."

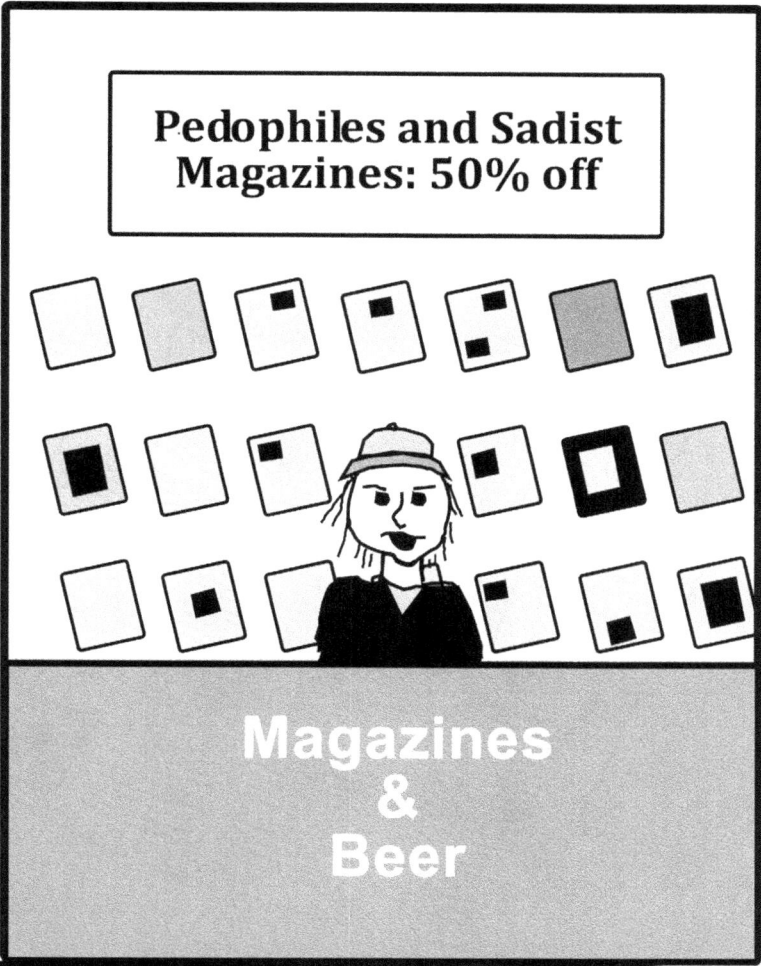

"This is so disgusting I don't even have words to describe how this came about."

"How about these words: Liberal interpretation of the First Amendment."

News of the World New York Blahblah Tuesday July X, 20YY

Neo-Nazis March Through Harlem: Riots Break Out

"Let me guess. The ACLU fought for the right of the Neo-Nazis to march through all Black neighborhoods. How come causing incitement to riot – like yelling 'fire' in a crowded theater – wasn't considered a factor?"

"Seems like a lot of things the ACLU does is a riot."

126

"What I don't understand about the Libs
who fight so hard to save forests: Why do
they build their houses out of new wood?"

"Gotta match their heads."

"Guess he's an old retired Liberal tree hugger."

"Yep ... old habits die hard, if at all."

"Now I really am confused. Aren't so many of these people owners of those idiotic specialty designer dogs that have been bred with so many problems they live lives of abject misery?"

"I guess they don't kick them."

"Must be a Yuppie Lib. No Conservative would be caught dead with one of those dogs."

"If they were it would be from fright."

"There's a taxpayer supported college that charges $30,000 a year."

"Haven't college costs risen at more than five times the inflation rate in the last twenty-five years?"

"Right ... can't beat the value of Liberal run education."

"I found out that once tenured, faculty members barely teach any courses and just spend their time on their own private research."

"Worse than that they take time out to lead rallies against US policies in the world."

"As you said: can't beat the value of Liberal run education."

"We as a nation waste, waste, waste. We have to take our position as citizens of the world seriously and learn to conserve."

"You know what's funny about this?"

"Indulge me."

"Nearly everyone in the crowd is holding a plastic bottle of water and each one came alone in his or her own car."

"Consider me indulged."

"The wars in South Uunga, Omumbaland and Quasiquasi have intensified ..."

Liberal News Network

"Why are we supposed to care about those places and why do we keep hearing about them?"

"Nobody ever heard of them until last week when the Libs found out there are starving kids there. Now they are screaming for the USA to bomb the place."

"Won't that just kill civilians and destroy what infrastructure they have and starve more people?"

"Yeah, but think of the children."

"The people are finally rising up against those hideous bugs."

"Sorry ... that's a crowd of Liberals rushing to herd and then hug them to protect them from harm."

"Well, shows the Liberals are good for one thing. They'll kill those bugs with love."

"Look at all those people carrying food and blankets and helping all of those people in need."

"So, you are going to say Liberals are do gooders after all?"

"Not really. This was the poorest, most destitute community in the country and people were barely making it, nearly starving from day to day."

"So the tornado ..."

"Gave the Libs a purpose."

Genetic Research for a Super Tomorrow

"Isn't genetic research supposed to be curing our worst diseases? What's the purpose of three-headed sheep?"

"This research may give the world a breakthrough: three-headed Liberals."

"Of course! Each one will spend so much time arguing with himself they'll leave the rest of us alone."

"Man do you catch on fast."

137

"I'm handing out flyers explaining why you need to support Liberals in every election coming up ..."

"I represent the Society to Save Everything and have this petition asking people to support saving the hissing cockroach from extinction ..."

"Ah, yes ... If they are not marching in rallies, Liberals are petitioning or handing out position flyers."

"I suppose ... but these are usually petitions or flyers that end up in rallies."

Gasp!

Wheeze

Huff!

Puff ... puff!

Whewwww!

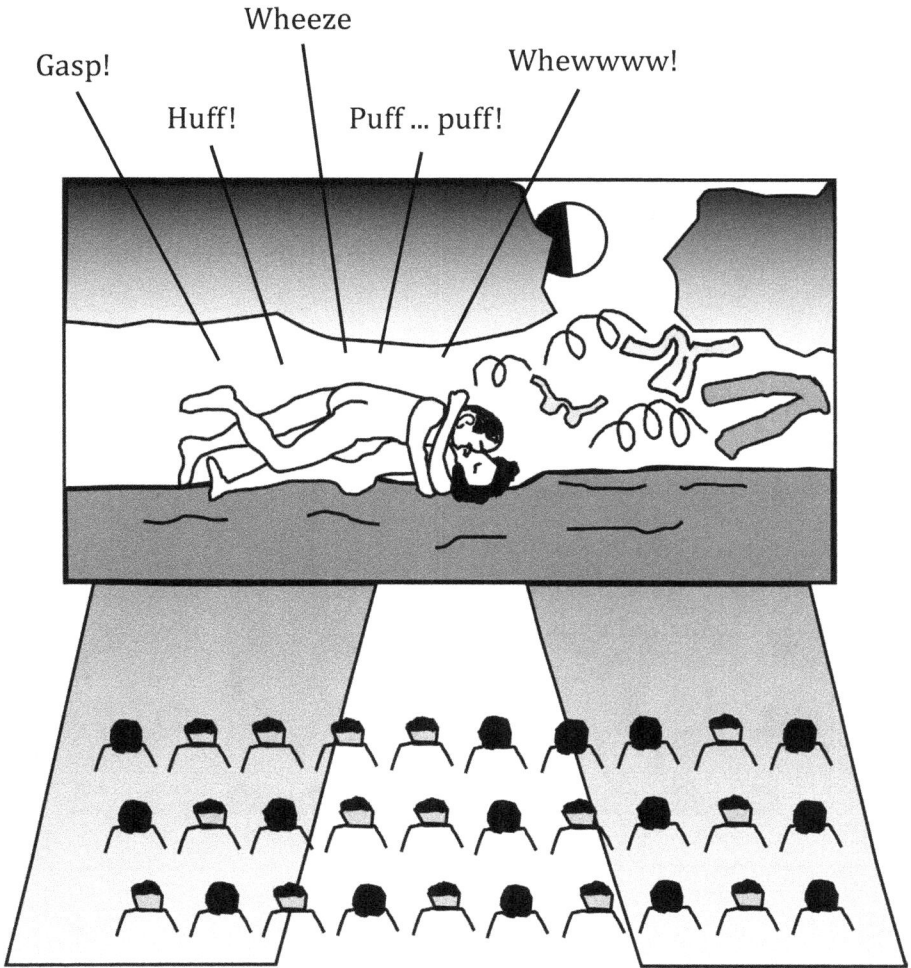

"How come all sex scenes in Hollywood show people frantically ripping off their clothes and immediately totally out of breath."

"Well, Libs are usually badly out of shape and clothes ripping during sex is probably the only exercise they ever get."

139

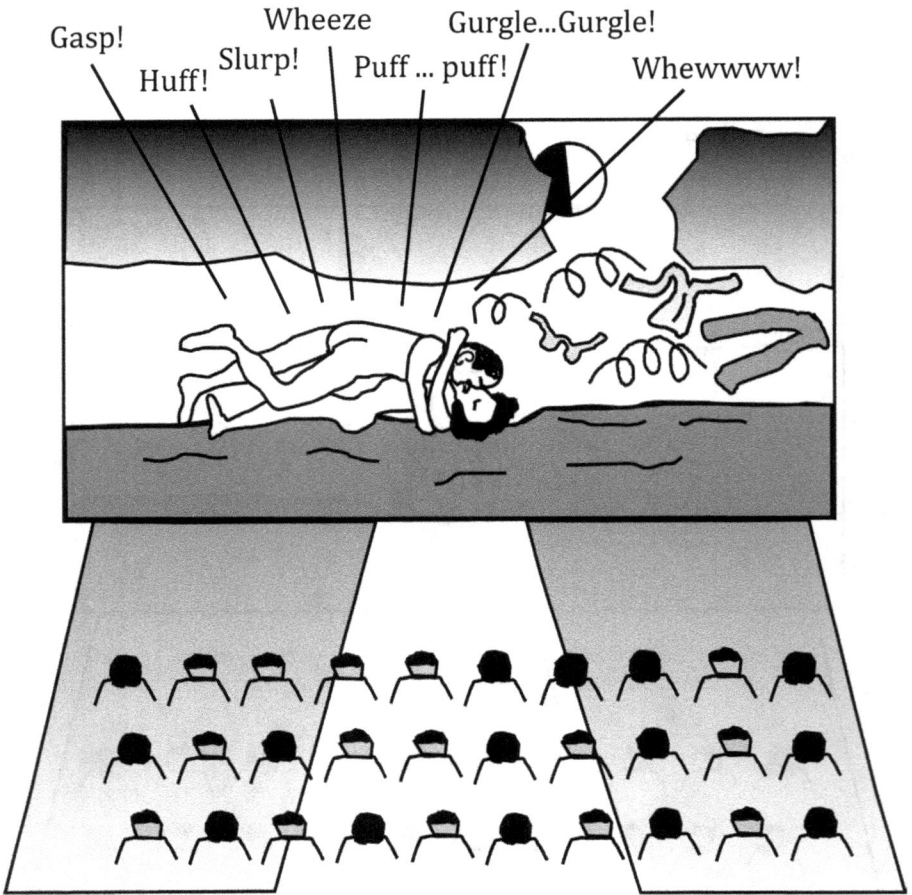

"It'll never cease to amaze me how brutal and unattractive sex is in Hollywood movies. The act never lasts more than a minute and people pant frantically in each other's faces after tearing each other's clothes off."

"I think you just summarized Liberal action: Run into the street, scream like crazy, push your face into your opponent's, and huff into his face,"

"What about the clothes tearing?"

"That's replaced by sign ripping."

"We have to control guns. We must stop the NRA. The NRA doesn't want any limit on guns!"

Blah Blah

"Explain something to me. The Liberals are always screaming about all kinds of curbs on the Second Amendment, but when it comes to speech they want no controls at all ... hate speech, vile defamation, incitement to riot, threatening death ... anything."

"That's why Liberals want gun controls, so when they incite to riot and threaten someone they won't get shot."

141

"Well, as you know, Kay, we Progressives have long understood that if only 38% of the people making between 90% and 99% of disposable income would just allow an increase of 6% to the 12% they already allow 45% of the time, then we could increase 11% of our revenue another 14% which would lower taxes by 18% for those in the 15% bracket while ..."

Liberal News Network

"I'm glad the Progressives understand this."

"What makes you think they do?"

Drone Air Strikes on Muslims Creating Hatred for America

News of the World   New York Blab   Tuesday July X, 20YY

"Don't these people already hate our guts and want to kill us so that's why we are bombing specific targets?"

"Don't tell the Libs that. They believe if we just let them attack us the Muslim World will learn to love us."

"At least they'll all learn to love attacking us."

"How come whenever Liberal TV has commentators talking about politics, finance or technology they always have the most bizarre and wacky British accents. Aren't Liberals always crowing about how they represent the best America can be"

"For some reason to Libs British means authoritive. And I suppose using a stuffy, snobby sounding foreigner to explain America's achievements proves just how much faith Liberals have in America."

"When did Liberals start calling themselves Progressives?"

"When they progressed to total irrelevance."

"That's so cute. Where are those items going? To a children's hospital to cheer up terminally ill kids?"

"Don't be silly. Let our kids fend for themselves. The Libs are sending that stuff to Arab Muslim countries to get their kids to love America."

"How adorable. Hope it doesn't clash with the Death to America clothing insignias they are taught to wear."

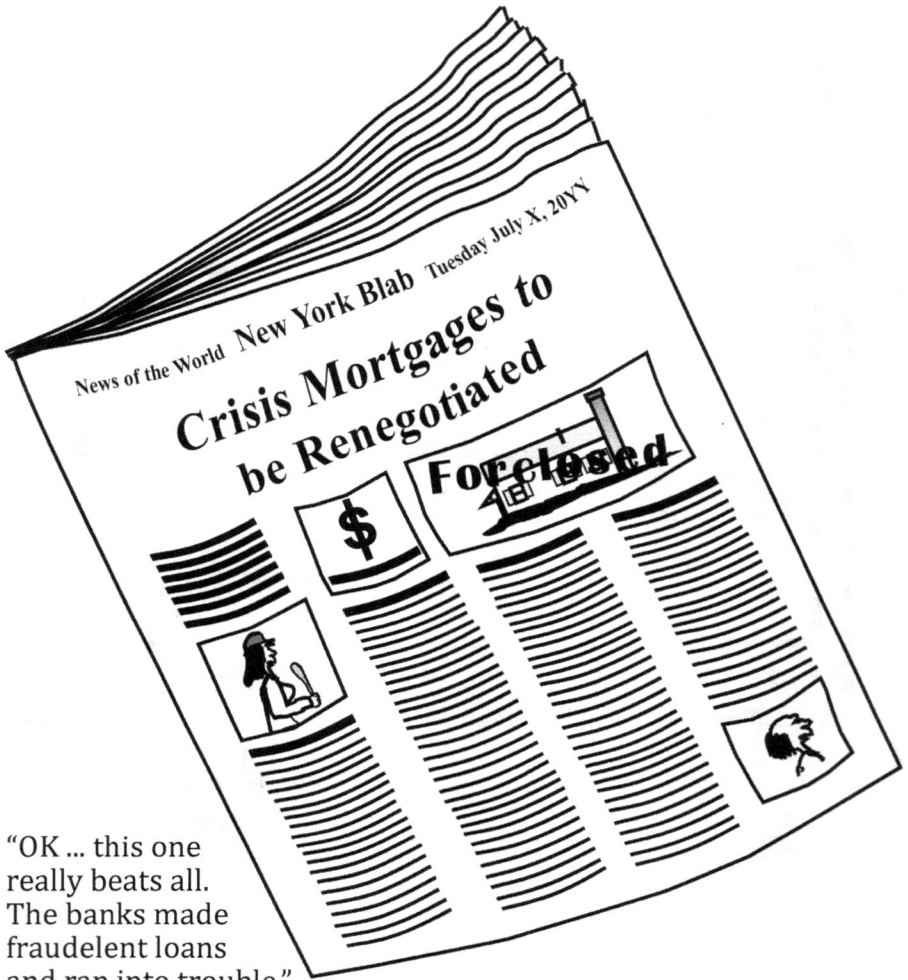

"OK ... this one really beats all. The banks made fraudelent loans and ran into trouble."

"And we taxpayers had to bail them out, no srings attached."

"Sure ... now the people who had no income, but bought $500,000 houses are being allowed to renegotiate their mortgages."

"And we taxpayers are being asked to bail that one out, too."

"With all this bailing out by us, who's gonna bail us out when the time comes?"

"Any taxpayers who are left."

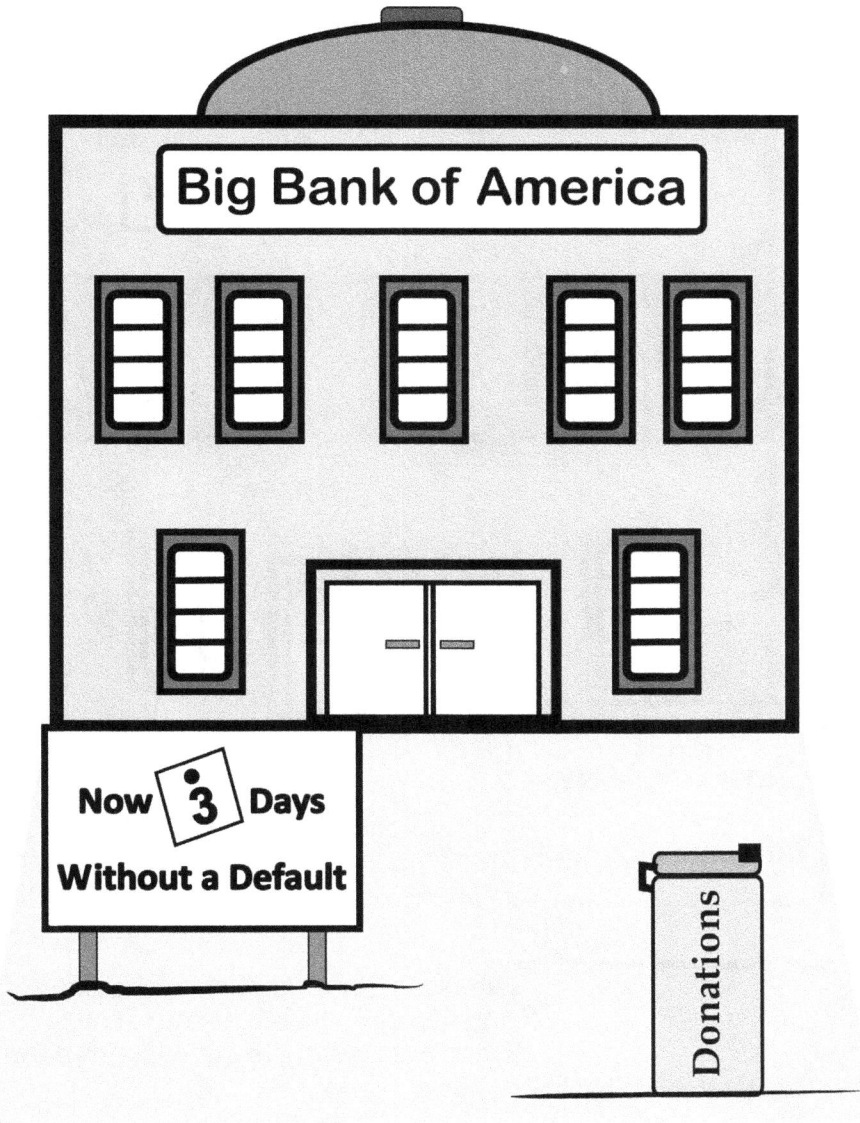

"Seems to me the efforts by the Progressives are starting to pay off."

"Uhhhh ... I think bankers realize Libs have no sense of irony."

149

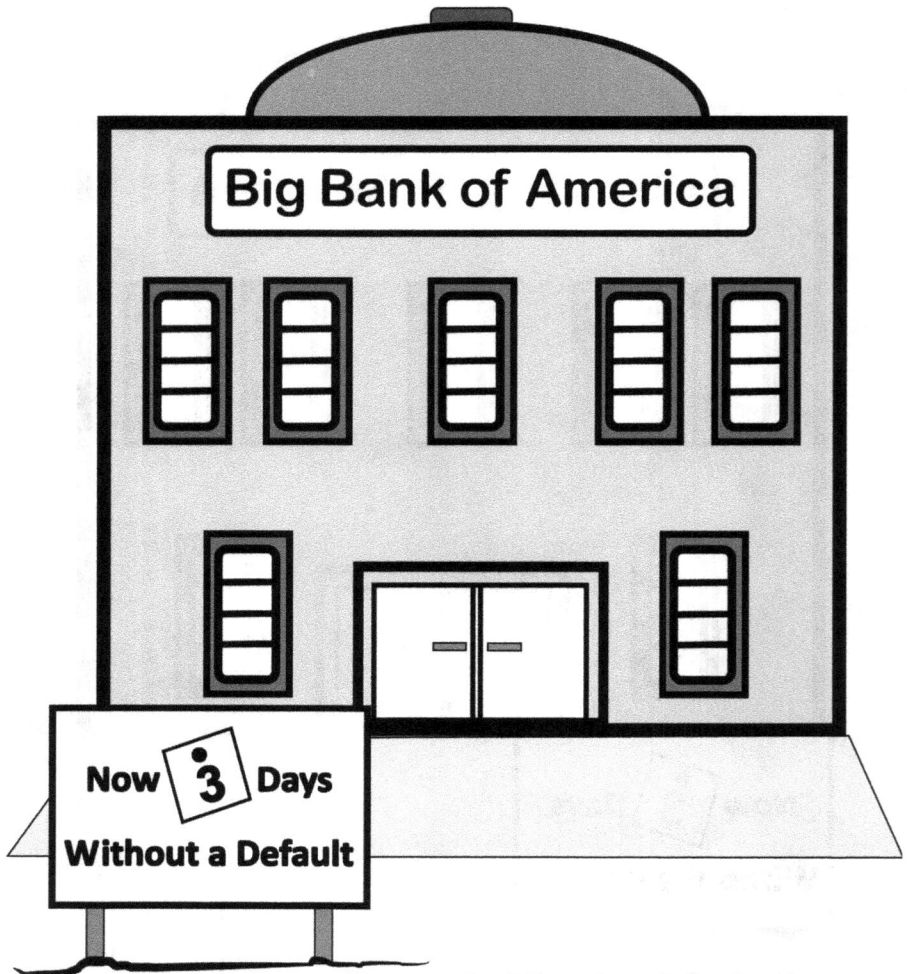

"I guess the Liberal push for banking controls after the big default swaps disaster is starting to get some traction."

"No ... the Liberals have simply switched their effort to fraudulent 'Days Without a Default' signs."

"How's that going for them?"

"Not so good. The Libs want a sign stating how many days have gone by without a sign."

"I can't wait for the Senate to pass a non-binding resolution on that."

Sen. Rob Glob (D)

Liberal News Network

"I understand that about 90% of all radio and TV talk and interview shows are Conservative."

"This leaves some 10% of the airways left over for the Liberals."

"But what do the Liberals do with that time? With a nine-to-one ratio of air time in favor of the Conservatives aren't the Liberals upset?"

"Of course they are, but that little bit of air time is plenty for them to do nothing but complain about what the Conservatives are doing with the other 90%."

"We have here Scrawl Screed, head of the Progressive Progressives for a Progressive America. Mr. Screed, you have complained about the Conservatives' name calling against Liberals."

"That's correct, Kay. As we in the Progressive Movement have long said Conservatives are nothing but scumbag terrorists who try to force their zealotry, bigotry, hatred for the poor on the rest of us and who promote their desire to destroy the American economy to feed their own selfish greed. In addition, their arrogance, self-righteousness, poisonous vitriolic hate speech and outright lying is beyond anything this country has ever known."

Liberal Week in Review

"I have no comment."

"Why bother ... he has enough for both of us."

"We Progressives have many ideas to promote a healthy economy and get everyone back to work. Our tax policies and wealth redistribution will ..."

"I have an interesting thought. Thousands of jobless Liberals pour into these rallies, right?"

"And your thought is?"

"If the wealthy Libs would just pay rally goers even a minimum wage, wouldn't that create a vast sea of ongoing jobs?"

"Spoken like a real Conservative."

153

"Who are those people? Must be hundreds in the last fifteen minutes alone."

"Those are lobbyists plying their trade on the Congress."

"Hold it ... don't the Democrats constantly complain about the influence of thousands of lobbyists? So why do they keep meeting with them."

"Because the Democrats keep belly aching about creating jobs."

"Huh?"

"How would it look if they put thousands of people out of work?"

"Look at that group of Good Samaritans who have rushed over to help those accident victims."

"Sorry to burst your bubble, but they're lawyers trying to elbow each other out of the way."

"How did they get there so fast?"

"They fly on the backs of buzzards."

"Yippee."

"Wow, that guy is sure happy. He must have been aquitted after being wrongly accused."

"Not true. He murdered three people in cold blood."

"B-but ... h-how did he g-get off?"

"His lawyer there kept putting in so many delays, writs and jury and witness challenges that by the time the case finally came to trial all of the witnesses had died and the evidence went moldy."

"Yep ... best justice money can buy."

"And Liberals fight to the death to keep it that way."

"Boy ... the Liberals must really be happy about this scene."

"What do you mean?"

"Well, here we have the very poor and the homeless gathered together in one place."

"I get it. Where else can you find a scene where people who need so much help are in one place, so the Liberals can just make one stump speech and pass one non-binding resolution in Congress?"

"No. Think of all the money they can ask for this place."

"Yeah ... just that much more money to send to Africa on behalf of these folks."

"That has to come after the mandatory part of the allocated money has been wasted on graft and corruption."

157

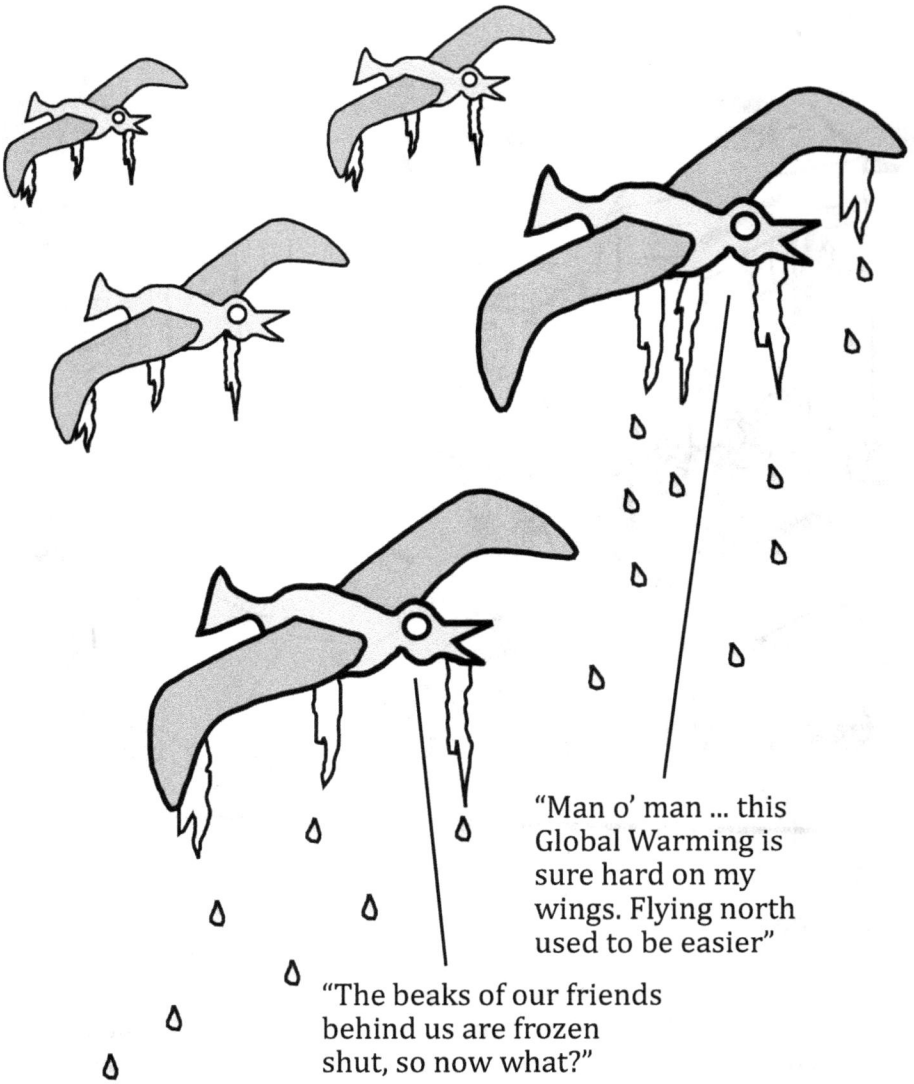

"Man o' man ... this Global Warming is sure hard on my wings. Flying north used to be easier"

"The beaks of our friends behind us are frozen shut, so now what?"

"They'll be OK."

"Why?"

"The Liberals complaining on the ground may make enough hot air to get us all home."

"This Global Warming is really getting bad. Last year only our wings were frozen over on our trip north. Now we have ice growing on our ice."

"We do have a Plan B."

"What's that?"

"The Libs keep saying Global Warming is getting worse, so next year we'll have ourselves shipped north in FedEx freezer containers."

New York Blab — Tuesday July X, 20YY
News of the World
NYC Incentive Funds:
The UN Building Being Torn Down to Build a Slum
Foreclosed
$

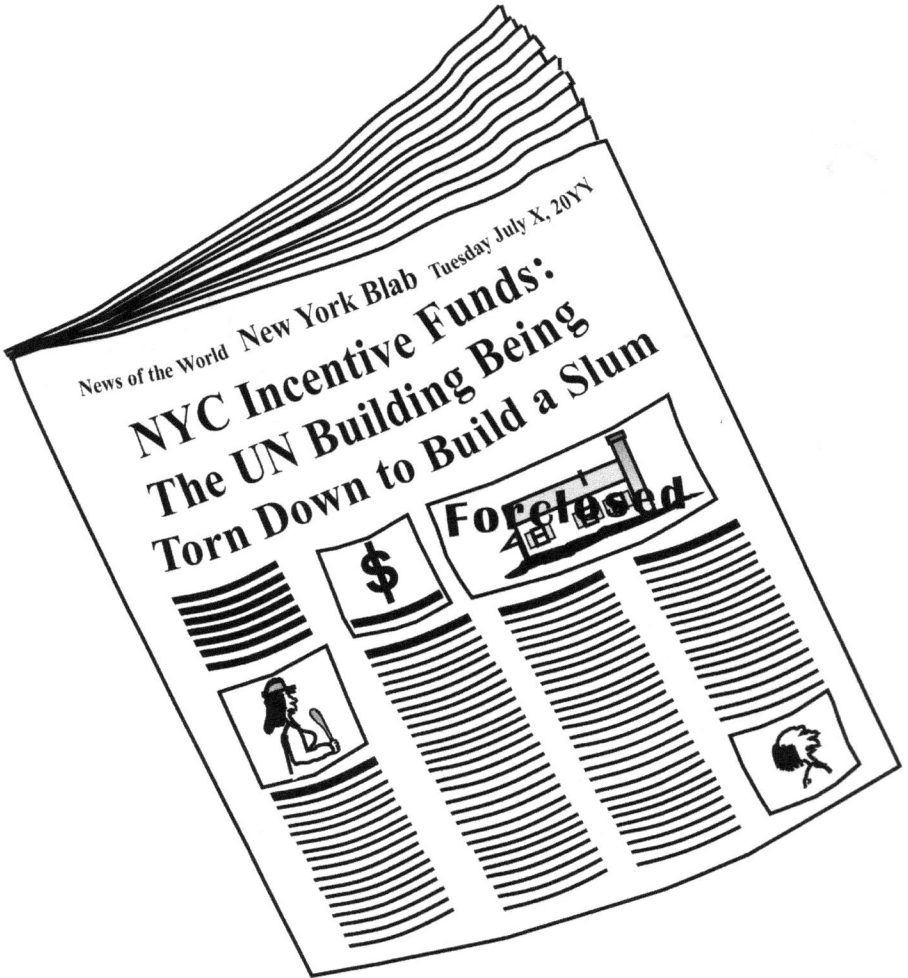

"That's too bad. The UN does have all anyone can want. It has an internal human rights organization with some of the world's most vicious dictators and it partners with outside groups who share their views. It has peacekeeping armies that allow free flow of arms to the countries wanting war while restraining the victims. It has a vast aid machine that just flows money to the dictators while the people starve. It declares war on Western values and supports rape of national resources the world over."

"Basically you are saying the UN is a Liberal's dream: so long as it supports the radical Left it is good. So building a slum will put them back at square one. Good move on New York's part."

"Wow ... What's going on?"

"This is how the Liberals solve pest problems: bring in or create a natural enemy. In this case birds with fifty foot wingspans had to be specially developed."

"Uhhhh ... So how are we supposed to control the huge birds?"

"The Lib scientists are working on thirty ton cats."

161

"Why are there so many dead people over there?"

"Well, the Liberals finally succeeded in eliminating every and all animal testing from all drug development."

"So what method are we supposed to use to determine whether or not a drug is safe?"

"You're looking at it."

"Welcome to Hard Head on M Mess NBC. All the Conservative candidtates for president of the United States took an oath to not raise revenue until the several hundred billion dollars in graft, corruption, waste and all the misguided programs that have done absolutely nothing to help anyone are eliminated. We have our Progressives panel to discuss just how foolish and imprudent this effort is and how all of us are going to be affected by this craziness ..."

HARD HEAD on M Mess NBC

"Well, sir. I think I'm gonna cut out of here while I still have some brain cells working."

"Hey ... kill the remaining ones to level the field with the Liberals."

163

YOUR LIBERAL MEMO PAD: Add your experiences with Liberals for future reference in case things get boring.

For Example: *On Tuesday, July 9th, I went to a convenience store and there was a strike taking place. Or a bunch of people were picketing. I asked one of the picketers what was happening. He told me that things weren't convenient enough. I asked him how long they were gonna inconvenience themselves. He walked away.*

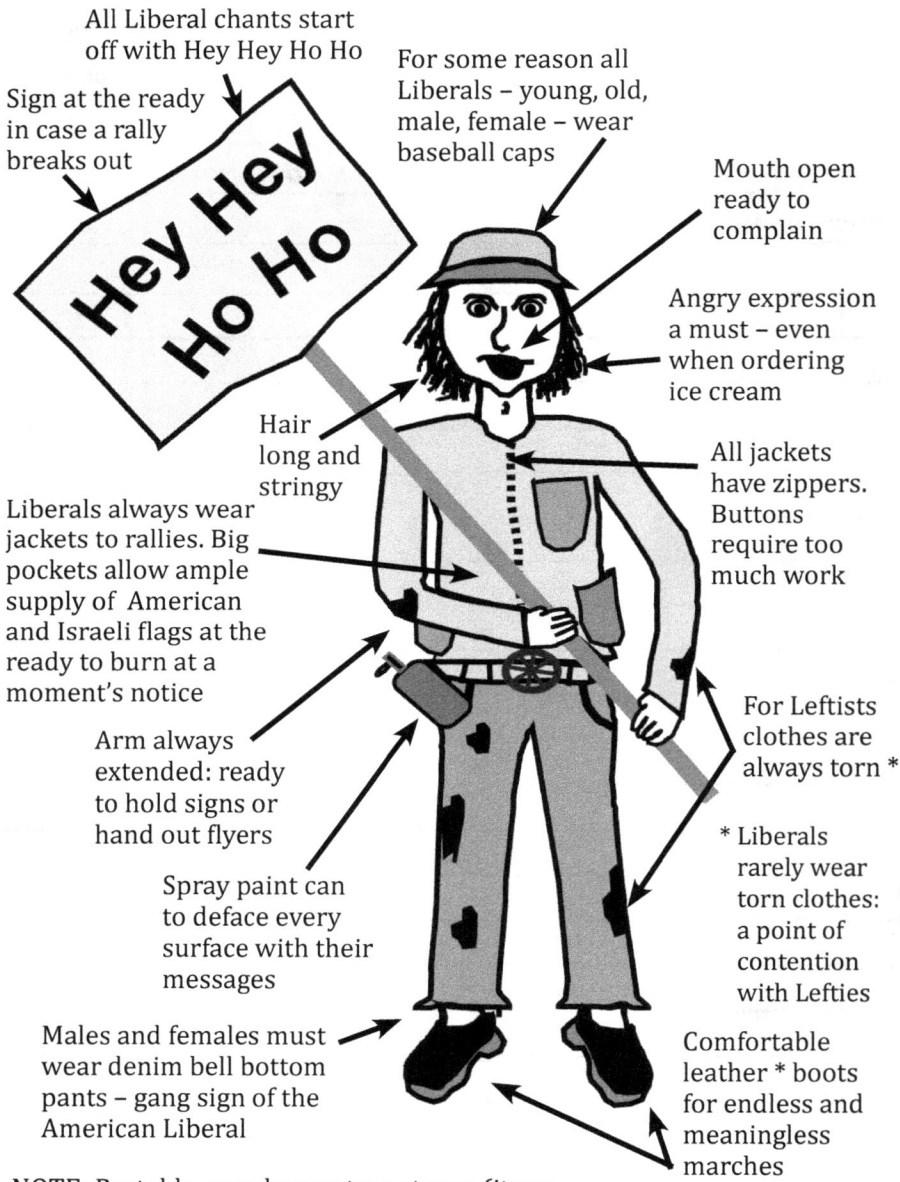

Features of the True American Liberal

All Liberal chants start off with Hey Hey Ho Ho

Sign at the ready in case a rally breaks out

For some reason all Liberals – young, old, male, female – wear baseball caps

Mouth open ready to complain

Angry expression a must – even when ordering ice cream

Hair long and stringy

Liberals always wear jackets to rallies. Big pockets allow ample supply of American and Israeli flags at the ready to burn at a moment's notice

All jackets have zippers. Buttons require too much work

Arm always extended: ready to hold signs or hand out flyers

For Leftists clothes are always torn *

* Liberals rarely wear torn clothes: a point of contention with Lefties

Spray paint can to deface every surface with their messages

Males and females must wear denim bell bottom pants – gang sign of the American Liberal

Comfortable leather * boots for endless and meaningless marches

Hey Hey Ho Ho

NOTE: Portable soap box or tree stump (items not shown) are optional and are for self proclaimed leaders. True leaders use podiums and microphones and are selected by his or her own proclamation

* Boots must be leather: emphasizes hypocrisy about animal rights

www.ingramcontent.com/pod-product-compliance
Lightning Source LLC
Chambersburg PA
CBHW050124280326
41933CB00010B/1243